Loft
living

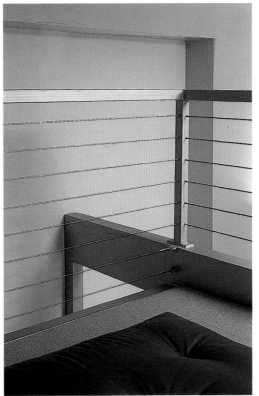

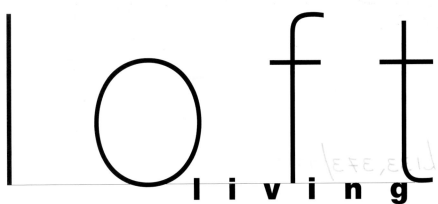

Loft
living

peggy
vance

CASSELL
ILLUSTRATED

to Sky and Biba Kang

First published in the UK 1999
This edition published
2003 by
Cassell Illustrated
Octopus Publishing Group
2-4 Heron Quays
London E14 4JP

Distributed in the United States by
Sterling Publishing Co., Inc.
387 Park Avenue South
New York NY 10016-8810

British Library Cataloguing-in-Publication Data
A catalogue record for this book is available from the
British Library

ISBN 1 84188 071 X

Designed by Roger Daniels
Edited by Caroline Ball
Plans by Amanda Patton
Printed and bound by Toppan Printing Co., (H.K.) Ltd.
Hong Kong

contents

Introduction

Today, loft living has become glamorous. It is associated with youth, freedom and the enjoyment of life. Suburban clutter is abandoned and the pure, clean lines of former industrial spaces embraced. Soaring double-height, open-plan areas are minimally furnished with a few modern design classics, leaving a sense of space and vast expanses of floor available for impromptu parties.

This is the popular image of a 'loft' apartment, and while – broadly speaking – it is an apt description, lofts today cannot be assumed to have any single look or style. The examples in this book are as various as the people who live in them, and the common strands that define loft living more subtle than one might imagine.

The increasing diversity of the loft look may be due in part to a broadening of the definition. Where once only the conversion of the top floor of an urban industrial space qualified for the description, now purpose-built loft apartments and even 'loft houses' are included within the genre.

Rebel Homes   Some modern lofts – architect-designed and in prime locations – are worth millions, a far cry from the budget appeal of the first lofts that appeared in the SoHo area of Manhattan as early as the 1940s. Essentially, these were studios so large that the artists who used them found it convenient just to move in, though they had to hide their residency from the authorities as it was in breach of the municipal planning and zoning regulations. Like all prohibitions, this made loft living, if not comfortable then at least subversive. For Andy Warhol and other New York artists it was a finger up to apple-pie notions of home and domesticity. Loft living was a quintessentially urban phenomenon, suited to a Bohemian, party lifestyle in which comfort and décor were not priorities.

In the dense urban environment of downtown New York, former industrial units offered space and light at budget prices. But the pioneering spirits who first moved into these very basic studios would be amazed by the architect-designed homes that are today described as 'lofts'.

Widening Appeal   By the 1960s the central location and sheer space available in downtown New York broadened the appeal of loft living to an urban middle class who could make the imaginative leap required to bridge the notions of factory and home. The cast-iron buildings that had accommodated light industry, such as printing and clothing companies, began to become desirable properties so that, by the 1970s, people started to accept the idea of buying an apartment for its square footage rather than its number of bedrooms.

Then, in September 1972, the British *Daily Telegraph* observed: 'The agony and expense of finding somewhere to live in the centre of two of the most crowded and expensive capital cities is forcing people to adopt extraordinary solutions.'

Based on the American model, loft living had arrived in London.

Rebirth of London Docklands In the early seventies the architect Tony Goddard converted Oliver's Wharf near Tower Bridge into shell spaces (see Penthouse Sweet, pages 18–29), and the developer Rae Hoffenberg refurbished a wharf in Limehouse to be sold as finished apartments. Whereas the focus of residential loft living in New York was disused factory buildings, in London the Thames-side wharves offered the greatest potential for conversion, with fine eighteenth- and nineteenth-century warehouses presenting vast spaces, stunning riverside views and a relatively central location.

From the seventies onwards more and more of these wharf warehouses have been recycled for residential use, a process that continues today (see Reservoir Docks – the Port East development, pages 121–9). In fact, the vogue for loft living is largely responsible for the current regeneration of the Docklands and the now thriving urban scene that has developed there. Many cities have looked to London and followed suit. In Boston the wharves have been similarly regenerated, and as far away as Australia, life on the waterfront has been changed forever by the advent of loft conversions.

The Developers Move In By the eighties a number of developers were specializing in the creation of lofts, and in London the Manhattan Loft Corporation (see pages 111–29), MetroLoft (see pages 52–9 and 140–9), London Buildings (see pages 131–9), Marylebone Warwick Balfour (see pages 122–9) and Sapcote (see pages 82–101) have become big players in this important new housing trend.

It is principally these developers who have translated a need – for large and exciting urban homes – into a product directed at the affluent and design-conscious. As Harry Handelsman, the charismatic chief of Manhattan Lofts, has remarked, 'We weren't selling property, we were selling lifestyle.'

Architectural Interiors   Today the architect- or interior-designed loft has really taken off. Clients buy shell spaces and then have the interior professionally laid out, decorated and even furnished. The resulting homes are often beautiful, spectacular and comfortable, though to some extent still frowned upon by the original loft dwellers with their DIY solutions.

But, as the architect-designed lofts featured in this book demonstrate, this development is far from being a degradation of the loft aesthetic. In designing loft conversions, most modern architects are particularly sensitive to the function and materials of the original buildings and, without exception, those whose work is seen here have sought a creative fusion between old and new. If well judged, the addition of mezzanine platforms, flexible 'room divisions', and functional design detailing contributes to the drama of the original space, and the introduction of new materials complements the look of the old.

The involvement of architects has led to even greater diversity in the look of contemporary loft interiors. Minimalism, though still the prevailing style, is now less of an orthodoxy, with whitewashed walls, exposed metal, sheet glass and huge expanses of hard flooring often being combined with, or giving way to, more interpretive treatments. Architects look back, not only to the lofts of downtown New York and the early Thames-side wharf conversions, but to architectural precedent in the work some of the greatest modern architects: Le Corbusier, Lubetkin (see The High Life, pages 30–41) and Mies van der Rohe, who explored space, light, circulation and function in new and radical ways.

In New York, inner-city industrial buildings have provided the principal stock for lofts, but in London it is the vast network of disused riverside warehouses. As a result, New York and London lofts are intrinsically different in their materials, proportions and location.

Homes of the Future   Every loft is different. There is no single loft solution, but we have reached the point at which lofts are the ultimate urban homes: spacious enough to relieve the tensions of cramped city life; reassuringly tied to the past but comfortably adapted to the present; and of a style that is both practical and chic. As many urban spacemen and women will attest, loft living can be truly life-changing.

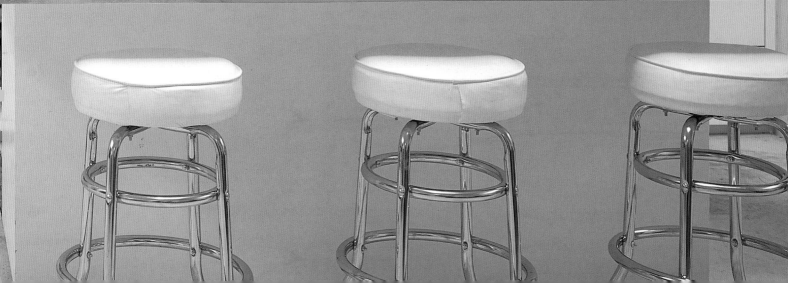

A derelict New York power station turned family loft, lit up with bright hues inspired by children's toys

loft original

Children can change your life. The New York architect, Walter Chatham, didn't realize how true this statement was until the arrival of his three kids – who totally changed his work. Having been happy with monochrome schemes, glass doors and the other trappings of modernism in the Big Apple, he began to question these orthodoxies as his own needs started to shift from those of an urban singleton to a family man.

Search for Space Accommodation is notoriously squeezed in Manhattan, so how to house three children comfortably in the city is a distinct challenge. A property that has been on the market for fifteen years without finding a buyer may not be everyone's ideal, but for Walter – who has extensive experience of the renovation of all sorts of buildings across America, from an airport terminal to a tea room – the conversion seemed to be more than just a possibility.

Sixteen years ago, Walter and his wife, Mary Adams Chatham, moved to an apartment in SoHo, an area where, at that time, rents were relatively cheap and space more plentiful than elsewhere in New York (in fact, the site of the first lofts in the city). When the children arrived, the Chathams bought the floor above and connected

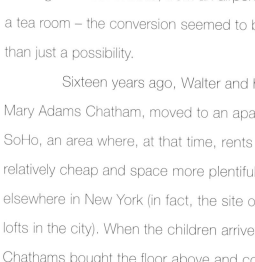

Few lofts have the benefit of greenery, but the roof of this converted New York power station provides a leafy, full-sized garden (above) easily accessible from the new iron stairway in the main living area (right).

the two storeys by elevator. But soon a desire for more integrated living led them to start searching for the ultimate loft. They looked at many renovated industrial spaces, but settled on the one that was the least habitable – in fact, a complete wreck. As Mary euphemistically says, 'We chose this space because it wasn't touched at all; it was totally pure.'

An abandoned SoHo power plant, the building conformed completely to the first tenet of true loft living by being an industrial space. The Chathams were more than happy with this, but equally concerned to create an environment that would be pleasant and convivial for the children.

The Chathams'
loft, planned
around a large
central living
space, has a
'children's zone'
at one end and
Walter and Mary's
bedroom at the
other, with stairs
leading up to
the roof.

STUDY

BEDROOM

MAIN BEDROOM
(studio above)

STAIRS
to studio and
roof garden

LIVING AREA

HALL

IN

BEDROOM

BEDROOM

Primary Palette   The most striking feature of the resulting loft is its use of colour, which is both chic and architecturally satisfying and, at the same time, appropriate to children's marked preference for light, bright interiors. As Chatham says, 'Living with our children is teaching me to operate more intuitively. Colour and light are the most joyful aspects of architecture.'

The scheme is undoubtedly exuberant. The staircase that links the main living floor to the upper studio and rooftop terrace resembles the arm of a crane in its gradient and height. There is nothing at all domestic about its structure and certainly no detailing, yet it is one of the most eye-catching features of the apartment, being painted a vibrant orange – a hue more associated with the disparate worlds of industrial installations and kindergartens than family homes.

Colour-lined   The loft has a satisfying clarity. The walls are washed a brilliant white, but all recessed areas – the interior surfaces of the bookcases and shelving – have been painted in the saturated bright yellow and green of children's toys. The effect is light, fresh and, through the simple device of the colour-lined cupboards, highly unusual.

Clever permutations of a single design idea, such as colour-lined shelves (above and right), are particularly satisfying in lofts as they help give coherence to open-planned and interconnected spaces.

Display Backdrop   This colour emphasis makes for wonderful displays. The rows and rows of books, with their bright spines, create random patterns within the colour niches, and art objects such as the family of fine glass tazzas and the row of female torsos, are particularly noticeable and impressive against the acid lemon.

Within each area of the house this storage conceit has a different look. In the kitchen, the somewhat more recessive green background allows a varied collection of items to be displayed on the open shelving – an effect less formal than in the main living space.

Bathtime Fun   In the bathroom, the solution is particularly inventive, with mirror glass set into the back of the cupboards – a completely new spin on the traditional bathroom cabinet with mirror. So, a simple design conceit, but one of consummate architectural purity, is used throughout the apartment to give an appealing coherence to the look of the whole. Just as Walter's children like colouring in, so does he.

Industrial Skeleton Exposed

The indestructibility of a power plant is a quality that appeals to the Chathams. Walter has left the pipes and flues of the original building intact and exposed, and

Prominent original pipework establishes a look at once functional and fun. The tubular steel chairs echo the pipe and, with their bright canvas seats, contribute to the relaxed atmosphere of this child-friendly loft.

has furnished the apartment in keeping with their solid, geometric forms. The clean, long lines of the rectangular space are complemented by pure, hard surfaces: for example, the original concrete flooring; the deep, architectonic recess of the bedroom door; and the wide, laminate kitchen worktop. The angles and textures are those of a modern industrial space, and yet this apartment has a distinctly homely atmosphere, with soft, colourful rugs, bright pictures, and delightfully informal touches, such as the green canvas chairs at the dining table.

There are four bedrooms in this loft, but the architect has not allowed the family's need for privacy to interfere with the classic loft aesthetic of wide, open-plan space. This apartment is still recognizably one floor of a large industrial building with a central 'thoroughfare' that stretches for most of its length.

Play Zone In fact, the entire, 9m-long entrance hall doubles as a playroom, complete with a hanging bar and a basketball hoop. This is in the heart of what might be called the children's zone, with all three children's bedrooms leading off it – communal territory that both divides and unites their little, private dens. As the third of these is windowless, Walter has ingeniously inserted an interior window that gives a view into the kitchen. The effect is appealingly surreal but appropriate in the context of the playful design of this apartment.

The small study that leads off the main living area may have been intended for adult use, but is now also the domain of the children. The open-plan layout of the main space literally invites the kids to 'have the run of the place'. Dashing from one end of the loft to the other, they career straight in and on to their parents' bed, which, deftly positioned at the centre of one end of the apartment, allows Walter and Mary to 'survey their entire realm without getting up', as *House Beautiful* so neatly put it.

The Chathams' traditional-looking bed is a pivotal part of this loft's scheme, positioned to allow Walter and Mary to see right down the length of the apartment.

Antique Linen In this adult bedroom, the mood and the look are somewhat different. The whitewashed walls and colourful cupboards are here, but so too are decorative details unique to this space. The floor is of oak and painted with green stripes. The chequer-patterned dressing cabinet, of Mary's own design, resembles a traditional piece of eighteenth-century furniture, and – most distinctive of all – an antique bed is draped with white linen to theatrical effect. One gets the impression that this room represents a marriage of minds, Walter's architectural skill and Mary's design flair combining to create an unusual, hybrid interior.

Garden in the Sky Just outside the bedroom door, the iron staircase rises to the upper level, which comprises Mary's studio (little bigger than the principal bedroom) and an enormous rooftop terrace that is effectively a playground for the children. In contrast with the clean, urban look of the interior, this terrace has the atmosphere of a country garden. Decked with wooden planks and made lush and green by the many plants in containers, it invites the children to play and the adults to dine *al fresco*. A haven in the heart of the city, it completes an unusual loft that is industrial and intensely practical, but homely, chic and comfortable.

Lofts are not usually thought of as being ideal for children, but in this Manhattan masterpiece Walter Chatham has shown that, with care and thought, they can be far more appropriate and adaptable than many family houses.

Tall windows on to the roof terrace provide Mary's studio with the maximum natural light. In the heart of the city, the Chathams have created an almost rural rooftop garden.

An art-gallery home with the raw beauty of a warehouse, the luxury of a palace and the light of a greenhouse

penthouse
sweet

Originally a tea warehouse, Oliver's Wharf is small in comparison with industrial-scale warehouse schemes such as Port East (see pages 121–9), but nevertheless a distinctive and eye-catching landmark on the north bank of the Thames, just 400m east of Tower Bridge.

Victorian Grandeur   Built in the 1870s, this miniature St Pancras is a consummate example of Victorian Gothic, with gargoyles, mullioned Venetian windows and polychrome brick detailing of Ruskinian purity. The *folie de grandeur* of this eccentric, attractive building, and its central location, brought it to the attention of the architect Tony Goddard, who, by the early seventies, was becoming interested in the possibility of converting old warehouses for residential use.

The First Loft Conversion   Between 1970 and 1972 Goddard and his colleagues, Colin Phillips and Jeremy Sumner, completely renovated and rehabilitated Oliver's Wharf, converting the building into twenty-three flats, each of which was designed to be as open and flexible as possible, allowing adaptation according to the occupants' specific needs. These prototype shell apartments had their services – kitchens, bathrooms and lavatories – concentrated into a core area, allowing maximum freedom of design in the remaining space. Oliver's Wharf gave an early indication of the potential for development in the Docklands, and, on its opening in 1972, received much publicity as an important, avant-garde conversion. In January 1971 *The Sunday Times* commented on the advent of what is now thought of as loft living:

'These warehouse flats represent an intriguing solution to two problems. First, the fact that many house hunters are put off by the tiny amounts of space they are offered for their money, and by the regimented way in which most new houses are divided inside. Second, the problem of what to do with the hundreds of outdated multi-storey warehouses which are quietly

mouldering away in town centres all over Britain. The solution: put the first into the second.'

The flats were sold on a non-profit, cooperative basis at between £7500 and £12,000. Goddard himself occupied the penthouse, his 'extraordinary solution' (*Daily Telegraph*, September 1972) being to turn the 370m² space into a two-storey, two-bedroom apartment with appropriately unusual features, such as a swing hung from a beam in the main living area. In March 1972 *The Architect* observed: 'Future inhabitants [of Oliver's Wharf] consider themselves to be the leaders in a movement designed to make this area one of the most "original" in the city.' But at the time Goddard made only modest claims about this Wapping development, stating in an interview with the same publication that the conversion was a 'simple matter'.

The Affluent Arrive   Since the seventies the prices of the apartments in Oliver's Wharf have climbed vertiginously with the rise and rise of loft living, so that, by the late eighties, their occupants included captains of industry and international stars. Yet they have consistently attracted those with an interest in the arts. Indeed, Lord Palumbo, the former Arts Minister, owned this penthouse until the early nineties.

When the current occupant, Barry Sack, a businessman, architectural enamellist and art collector, bought this apartment in 1992, he was attracted by its potential as a gallery home – the perfect space in which to exhibit his exquisite collection of paintings, drawings, sculpture, textiles and, of course, enamel.

The Victorian Gothic architecture of Oliver's Wharf (opposite) suggests a dim and relatively low-ceilinged warehouse interior, but in this three-storey apartment (above) the architects have created soaring voids that send natural light deep into the space.

Faced with the daunting task of refurbishing what was effectively a stripped-out shell, he approached the relatively young architectural practice of McDowell + Benedetti, which, although only in its first year, had been shortlisted in the Bankside to St Paul's RIBA Millennium Bridge competition.

The Architects' Challenge Jonathan McDowell and Renato Benedetti were impressed by the Grade II listed building and captivated by the river views from the penthouse. On beginning the project, their starting point was a 250m² double-height space with a complex pitched roof supported on massive oak trusses and cast-iron stanchions. Their brief was to refurbish the interior completely, introducing mezzanine platforms and a rooftop conservatory and terraces that would increase the space to 400m². Additionally, their client had a very clear idea of his particular needs.

Barry's main desire was that the space be as open and undivided as possible in order to maintain the barn-like appearance of the roof. A dedicated cook, he wanted the kitchen to be in the centre of the apartment, allowing him to have easy communication when entertaining, and was keen that the architects should make the most of the dramatic views, maximizing the experience of the river.

A comparison of the ground plan (bottom) and a cross-section through the centre of the apartment (below) shows how the architects have extended the space from 250m² to 400m² though the introduction of mezzanine and terrace levels, with the limestone wall like a spine through the middle.

CONSERVATORY

TERRACE

BEDROOM

KITCHEN

GALLERY

MAIN STAIRS

GALLERY (double height)

SECRET STAIRS to mezzanine

LIVING AREA (single height with mezzanine above)

HALL (double height)

IN

BALCONY

LIVING AREA (single height with mezzanine above)

LIVING AREA (double height)

BEDROOM

Going with the Flow In tune with these objectives, the architects began work on a design that as far as possible avoided interrupting the flow of the existing space. On entering the apartment, for example, the galley kitchen offers a vista right through the heart of the flat to the principal window overlooking the river.

Kitchencentric Design   Designed in its entirety by McDowell + Benedetti, the kitchen, which comprises an open galley and enclosed scullery area, is finished throughout in satin-polished stainless steel. The apparent simplicity of the resulting effect gives the whole an industrial quality appropriate to Barry's practical approach to cooking. Indeed, the design of this apartment was worked out over lengthy, convivial dinner meetings for which he catered.

The attention to detail in the remodelling of this interior is nowhere more evident than in the kitchen: even the scullery sink was specifically designed to accommodate the especially large shelves of the Gaggenau oven. McDowell + Benedetti also worked on some small-scale practical

As requested by the client, architects McDowell + Benedetti designed the professional-quality galley kitchen (above and top) as an almost sculptural focal point of the lower level of the apartment.

innovations, such as the drying rack that, by means of a single diagonal steel strut, can accommodate every conceivable size of plate.

Behind the cooker, the stainless steel splashback is in fact a sliding screen that can be rolled away when not in use to reveal a new limestone wall that forms the main spatial division in the apartment. And the units, raised off the floor, seem almost to hang suspended in the air when sunlight floods in beneath them.

The Warm Wall   The limestone wall, which is McDowell + Benedetti's principal new introduction, runs like a spine down the centre of the space to the full three-storey height, extending into the open air at the level of the roof terrace.

This 20cm-thick wall determines the layout of all three levels of the apartment. At the lower level it defines a long gallery or hall space lined with the gems of Barry's art collection. The architects have even designed a display shelf into the wall so as to avoid the need for potentially unsightly and scarring fixings. And the limestone itself – finely honed and of a light but warm hue – has the quality of a Ben Nicholson painting, the abstract interplay of shape, level and texture creating an impression of calm, infinite space.

The fireplace is just one of the openings in this unusual firescreen, which, like a gleaming metal wall, visually connects the lower and mezzanine levels and conceals the stair to the mezzanine.

This apartment offers vistas in all directions. From the principal living area (above) one can see up to the apex of the beams. Even the steel and glass stairway (right) is free-standing so as not to interrupt the visual continuity of the warehouse shell.

The Secret Stair Extending across the width of the lower level, the sitting room is divided into summer and winter areas, the former occupying the west corner (which has two exterior walls) and the latter the more sheltered east corner into which McDowell + Benedetti have designed a highly unusual fireplace. This is effectively a square opening in a 10mm-thick steel-plate fireplace screen so large that it extends up into the mezzanine study area above and had to be welded on site. Again, this intervention – like a great steel sculpture – is kept at a distance from the brick wall to interrupt the original space as little as possible, and this allows the architects a dextrous sleight of hand: completely concealed behind the screen is a secret steel staircase to the mezzanine.

This small bedroom/study area is one of two separate open mezzanine platforms (the other supports the principal bedroom) and, with a huge pivoting window overlooking the river and furnished with a single chaise, is an intensely private space inviting relaxation and reverie.

Home Comforts Returning to the lower level, the kitchen opens on to a wide dining area with a circular table able to accommodate up to sixteen people. Beyond this public space, totally hidden from view, is a conventionally sized spare bedroom, which Barry calls the 'messy room' and has filled with homely clutter and possessions of sentimental value. Yet even in this single-height smallish back room the architects have been deft in their use of space, introducing a bed which folds up into the wall and an en suite shower that neatly divides two separate lavatories.

The Sculptural Stairs In a pyrotechnic display of architectural flare, McDowell + Benedetti have designed a free-standing stair up through the three storeys, linked to the mezzanine and roof levels by steel bridges. This stairway has almost the appearance of an altar at the end of the gallery, its central screen of cast-glass slabs naturally lit by the roof-light in daytime and by concealed uplighters in the floor at night. Around this great core of glass a zig-zag stair of shot-blasted steel elegantly climbs; like the other metalwork elements in the loft, it involved extensive site welding by Now First Limited.

Cast-Glass Features   Glass is an important feature in this apartment. As well as the stairwell centrepiece, the cast-glass artist Jeff Bell was commissioned to make the font-like wash basin in the principal bedroom, a free-standing shower screen in its en suite bathroom and the 'shark's fin' benches in the rooftop conservatory (which extend out on to the roof

Jeff Bell's cast glass objects – the bedroom basin (right), the core of the stairway and the benches on the roof terrace – are one of the visual leitmotivs of this apartment. Cast glass, with all its natural irregularities, emulates the texture of water so it is particularly appropriate for a river setting.

The mezzanine bedroom is like a great deck extending into the open air. The window is effectively a glass wall that slides back to unite inner and outer spaces.

terrace). As distinct from float glass, cast glass includes bubbles and textured surfaces that occur naturally in the process of firing, and is always finished manually to reveal the patina that is the equivalent of the grain in timber.

Glass details are particularly appropriate in Barry's mezzanine bedroom because a complete wall of glass is all that separates him from the elements. Even in the bathroom there is no window dressing to obscure the astonishing view of Tower Bridge, and although there is privacy enough from neighbours, Barry suspects that river travellers may be able to glimpse him in the shower.

Art and Colour   Behind the bed, one of Barry's enamel works creates a gently curving wall that, again, resembles an altarpiece, its two panels creating a modern diptych. The saturated colour of this work is balanced here by other strong hues: a rich Chinese-lacquer orange for the drawer and storage units; and what the architects specified as Yves Klein blue for the sliding bathroom door, but which when applied appeared more purple than anticipated. In the bathroom a small niche in the wall wittily accommodates a classical bronze and a bath duck, and is an echo of the other niches in the apartment: the hatch and recessed display shelf in the limestone wall, and the bookcases in the fire screen.

Reflecting the Elements   At the highest level – the rooftop – the elemental quality of this brick, wood, stone and glass apartment becomes even more pronounced, as does the architects' response to the external elements: light and water. On the lower levels, McDowell + Benedetti have created an interplay of vistas through the new and existing windows, using natural, blond surfaces as screens for water reflections.

Barry Sack's gently curving enamel panels are a key feature of the bedroom (right), inviting the use of other strong planes of colour, including the sliding door of the en suite bathroom (above). Solutions inspired by or incorporating fine art are a particular characteristic of this collector's loft.

At the upper level of the rooftop conservatory and terrace their aesthetic of 'truth to materials' – liberated from the practical constraints of services, fixtures and fittings – is given free rein. The limestone wall that is at the core of the apartment projects up and out of the original building to become the west wall of the conservatory. This steel and glass structure, despite being designed to have the same degree of curvature as original windows on the floors below, has a nautical look, and, like a great glass cabin, catches the morning and evening sun to port and starboard.

The rooftop of this old tea warehouse has been transformed by the addition of a shimmering post-modern conservatory that, like the bedroom below, unites interior and exterior spaces with a single deck.

Along both sides of this elegant roof room, cast-glass panels form continuous benches that extend out on to the roof terrace, where, in the sunshine, they resemble thick sheets of melting ice. With its panoramic views over London, sitting on this terrace feels like having reached the summit of a mountain. Barry has eschewed greenery at this level in favour of a collection of rocks and pebbles, this choice entirely in keeping with the leitmotiv limestone wall and the other natural raw materials in the apartment.

Challenges and Triumphs Both architect and client knew that the project would have its difficulties. The need for extensive construction work in a fully occupied building and for a scaffold platform to be built out over the river were obvious problems. Less apparent but equally taxing was the discovery of hazardous asbestos and the occurrence of freak rainstorms that caused extensive flooding, not just of this apartment but of others. But, amazingly, though the schedule lengthened, the work continued. The result is the realization of a dream: an art-gallery home with the raw beauty of a warehouse, the luxury of a palace and the light of a greenhouse.

the high life

**The great architect
Lubetkin's famous
Highpoint penthouse, a
seminal example of lofty
ideals at the highest
point of London**

The classicism of Highpoint, so deftly acknowledged in the caryatids supporting the entrance porch (below), is particularly apparent in the original ground plan of the penthouse and its terraces (bottom), which reveals a broadly symmetrical structure.

ighpoint is a familiar if incongruous landmark at the summit of London's Highgate Village. Designed by the Russian émigré Berthold Lubetkin, the great modern architect and leader of the Tecton architectural group, it rises like a sheer white cliff above the Georgian terraces of this quintessentially English area. A blue plaque records that Dickens was a visitor to a friendly looking cream-coloured house directly across the road, and A. E. Housman lived only a few yards away in a fine Georgian villa. By contrast, the two buildings that comprise Highpoint (Highpoint One and Two) are startling for their imposing scale and International Modern style.

A New Aesthetic   Lubetkin (1901–90) may not have thought of these apartment blocks as being 'International Modern' – details such as the neo-classical caryatids supporting the entrance porch ward off such a label – but there is no doubt that he was in the business of demonstrating a new aesthetic, and – strangely perhaps, given the wealth in Highgate – bringing the concept of social justice to British architecture.

Strange as it may seem now, these concepts were unprecedented in a country that previously solved housing need through the creation of cottage-style garden suburbs, and this flagship modern building attracted immense prestige in architectural circles though, equally, opposition from much of the local community. (Ironically, the Highgate Society, which was formed in reaction to Highpoint One, is now the most vigilant guardian of the buildings' conservation.) Undoubtedly, it would never have been built without the patronage of Sigmund Gestetner, whose office equipment firm was one of the most important employers in North London, and who was prepared to

give Lubetkin free rein in the design of a collective housing block – at this stage intended to provide homes for his employees.

Elevated 125m above sea level, the site purchased was very promising, despite the council's height restriction of 20m on the street frontage. The finished seven-storey building, though recognizably a product of the Modern Movement, was not dogmatically so. As Lubetkin was at pains to point out, 'We spared no effort to underline in "the red ink of the imagination" the exceptions to the diagram.' To this end, elements were inserted on the roof (a communal terrace) and ground floor (a lounge and tea room) as deliberate digressions

Around the open-plan core of this loft are moderately sized though not conventionally shaped 'rooms'. The main bedroom has a gently curving wall that echoes the vault of the living area's ceiling (see page 37), and has a similar effect in suggesting infinite space.

from the structural regularity of the floors between, and it in this spirit of digression that Lubetkin embarked on the design of Highpoint Two.

The Creation of Loft Apartments   By 1938, the relatively large flats of Highpoint One were principally occupied by the intelligentsia rather than Gestetner's workers, so that when the planning authority gave permission for the second block to comprise only twelve flats rather than the originally envisaged fifty-seven, the shift from

As seen in John Allan's original photograph, the apartments below the penthouse demonstrate Lubetkin's bold experimentation with double-height spaces and mezzanine platforms (above), both features being characteristic of today's loft apartments.

designing workers' housing to duplex apartments was not an insurmountable obstacle for the architect, although undoubtedly other factors also played a role in his decison to proceed. Essentially, Lubetkin knew that if he didn't build the more expensive Highpoint Two flats, then another architect would build something incongruous with Highpoint One. As Lubetkin's monographer, John Allan, observes, 'If Highpoint One could just sustain the metaphor of the Soviet Commune, Highpoint Two might be characterized as a Victorian mansion block.' Certainly these new apartments were created as luxury homes – complete with separate servant routes – but in the fusion between Lubetkin's thinking about utilitarian homes for Highpoint One and luxury apartments for Highpoint Two arguably a new housing concept evolved – the purpose-designed 'loft' apartment.

The Highpoint Two apartments reiterated the space-saving, flexible features of Highpoint One: built-in kitchens, communicating living and dining rooms and open-plan entrance areas – as well as introducing other features that today we readily associate with loft living, including double-height spaces, mezzanine galleries and glazed walls.

Like many more modern lofts, the penthouse offers easy communication between interior and exterior. The 7.5m glass wall (above) retracts to open up the entire length of the main living space to the terrace with its views over Highgate Heath and beyond.

The Penthouse   Lubetkin's own apartment – the penthouse of Highpoint Two – is the ultimate expression of the architect's willingness to experiment with a lofty aesthetic entirely of his own creation. The penthouse commands an astonishing 360-degree view that takes in the whole of London and the five counties surrounding it. The available roof space is divided between indoor and outdoor areas (in roughly equal proportions), though the distinction is broken down when the 7.5m glass wall in the living area opens to the elements the entire Heath-facing side of the apartment. Standing in this space, with the wind whipping your hair and making your clothes billow, the feeling of exhilaration is the same as when one is suddenly buffeted by a sea breeze.

The Drama of Arrival   Like many later lofts, the penthouse dispenses with a conventional room plan. The lift that rises from the graceful lobby arrives not in a faceless communal hallway, but into the apartment itself. Thus the first impression is of welcome – visitors prepare to enter, unaware that they have already arrived. This directness is deliberate

and sustained. Sliding the lift door aside, you are aligned to walk right into the main body of the apartment – indeed your entrance is invited by a visual corridor of blue-painted rafters that seem to prompt your advance. Within seconds you have been drawn into the grand central space of the main living area and the effect is breathtaking – a visual shift from the material to the ethereal.

Overhead, a vaulted blue ceiling is symbolic of the sky; underfoot, rich brown tiles stretch from wall to wall like a ploughed field; on the walls, sand-blasted pine panelling looks as rough and woody as a forest; and – open or closed – the glass disappears into the panoramic view of the landscape.

On stepping out of the lift, one feels drawn into the heart of the apartment (below), 'invited' to enter by the strong perspective effect of the floor tiles and the striation of the rafters that seem to signal advance.

Seasonal Spaces   In Lubetkin's time and today, these are the basic elements of the space. In this central core there are no rooms as such but areas that are transformable for different purposes. So, for instance, the wall of windows suggests a room area for summer sitting in relative openness. But, defined by a fireplace, low ceiling and a pillar, there is also a second living area which, though open to the first, has a distinct mood, as if the 'landscape' of the room had changed season from summer to autumn.

The Concrete Screen   Originally a third area, for dining, was defined by an unusual concrete screen that housed Lubetkin's collection of 'found' objects and divided the space without diminishing it. Though this has since been demolished, it was an important feature, the precursor of the many devices used in lofts to create virtual room spaces within an open-plan layout. In fact this tripartite room, with its three distinct but totally interconnected areas, has proved to be a template for much loft design.

Enduring Influences Today, without the screen, the space is vast, but still used in the same way. The penthouse is currently owned by the philosopher Erez Yardeni and the furniture designer Ou Baholyodhin. They are passionate about Lubetkin's original interior and, with John Allan of Avanti Architects, have reintroduced many features. From Lubetkin's daughter, Sasha, they have acquired two of the architect's highly unusual hide chairs that

Contemporary photographs of Lubetkin's own furnishings (top) show the screen, used for storage and display and to separate living from dining areas, that anticipated the room-dividing devices of modern lofts. Erez and Ou have reinstated the virtual dining area by siting Ou's Temple table and chairs where Lubetkin's fold-down table would have stood originally (left).

Lubetkin's original hide chairs (above) are in keeping with the rural symbolism of the apartment, and are also the ancestors of the low-slung casual furniture much used in modern lofts.

he specifically designed to encourage informal lounging (*de rigueur* in a modern loft). These may look rough-hewn and natural – in keeping with the rustic symbolism of the room – but are in fact very carefully constructed: Lubetkin chose to have the hides of different beasts invisibly stitched to create exactly the piebald effect he was after, but played on this patchwork idea by superimposing broad seams of coarse leather stitching. These chairs may appear a far cry from the smooth leather and steel furniture produced by many of Lubetkin's contemporaries, notably Le Corbusier, but are no less important in their influence on modern design. Low, wide seating is a norm in modern lofts, and the witty, piebald hide anticipates the kitsch furry fabrics often used for soft furnishings today.

The central living space, with its over-arching blue ceiling and window wall, is so vast and open that one might imagine it to be rather cold, especially as it is the highest and arguably the most exposed point in London. But here again, Lubetkin avoided modernist austerity through the addition of under-floor and under-ceiling heating, so that – as in modern lofts – the apartment can be made cosily warm, even in the depths of winter.

This modern classic, an Eames Chaise of 1948, complements the fluid curve of the white bedroom wall and is in satisfying contrast with the dark and angular West African sculpture.

An Art Space Erez and Ou consider that they are living in a work of art, and they have consciously avoided 'dumbing down' the architect's original vision. But, because of alterations made by previous tenants, the look today is less residential than when the penthouse was Lubetkin's home. The screen with its display shelves and the bookcases has gone, as have Lubetkin's strange decorations: an enlarged picture of an amoeba on the door between the hall and living area and the Pollock Victorian theatrical prints that used

to paper the outer kitchen wall. With the help of John Allan, Erez and Ou plan to reintroduce the screen, bookcases, amoeba picture and prints, and also the soft rug that can be seen in photographs of the original interior.

For Erez and Ou the uninterrupted space offers the perfect setting for a few, well-chosen pieces of furniture and art objects. Lubetkin's friends and contemporaries – Calder, Le Corbusier and others – visited the penthouse and gave the architect works of art that formed part of the overall effect. Taking the lead from Lubetkin's ability to integrate disparate elements to create something greater than the sum of the individual parts, Erez and Ou have combined a few pieces of Ou's own furniture – the Temple table and chairs and a Torii console table (outside the kitchen) – with other modern classics, including wooden Cherner chairs by Paul Goldman and a Sori Yanagi stool. The art is equally eclectic, but appropriate to the space. The

Today the penthouse houses a fine collection of disparate artworks. In the corner of the main living area a West African figure sits regally upon Ou Baholyodhin's Torii table, beneath a Constance Spry ceramic bowl – unlikely room-mates but none the less compatible.

couple's important collection of Constance Spry ceramics, back lit in the unusual ceiling niche, and objects from Erez's collection of West African art, are sited in key positions around the apartment.

Having previously lived in a country cottage, they found they had to shed about 80 per cent of their possessions on the move to Highpoint. When Erez's sister asked how he could be comfortable living in somebody else's strongly individual notion of a home, it struck him that if he were to commission a new home from a great architect, then the penthouse would closely match his expectations – and perhaps even surpass them.

In the entrance area a blasted pine bench offers a clear invitation to sit and contemplate a view semi-screened by hefty planks of the same wood. In this symbolic forest Lubetkin aimed to create an experience similar to sitting on a fallen trunk and watching the play of light through the trees.

Contrasts Off the main living area are smaller, more intimate rooms – a hallway, two bedrooms, two bathrooms and a kitchen – that offer a pleasing contrast to the vast central space. Yet these are no less impressive in their conception and detailing. The window in the hallway is semi-screened by vertical planks of the same scorched and sand-blasted pine used for panelling and the hide chairs – an unusual feature that anticipates the adventurous design solutions that distinguish lofts from more conventional homes.

Wit and Spirituality Lubetkin was a very witty architect, and the concealed door to the bathroom off the hall is a amusing conceit of just the sort that we expect in modern loft interiors. This humour and willingness to experiment make Lubetkin one of the greatest architects of the twentieth century and a father of modern loft design, but equally, his penthouse has been influential for its spiritual dimension, which is particularly apparent in the natural symbolism and the altar-like ceiling niche. Loft design today is not about carving up converted spaces, but about finding new, less constrained ways of living – both practically and spiritually.

Changing Lives When the Ou and Erez first saw the penthouse they were captivated. Ou observes, 'We never dreamt we'd end up buying it, but once the lift doors opened and we came face to face with this, we knew that whatever it took – arms, legs, eyes – we had to have it.' Rarely do people feel like this about conventional flats and houses, but loft living is a passionate business. To want to dwell in an open and unusual space you have to be a bit open and unusual yourself. 'People often ask us what it is like to live somewhere so individual,' says Erez. 'But we feel it was made for us. And it's had a huge impact on the way we live.' As the caretakers, curators and partakers of the penthouse, the couple have recognized Lubetkin's almost clairvoyant anticipation of modern trends, and have preserved this unique home as a testament to the architect's seminal vision.

In creating his own bespoke 'loft', Lubetkin was far from austere. The décor, fixtures and fittings have been updated (below), but this enclosed yet generous bathroom invites sybaritic pleasure.

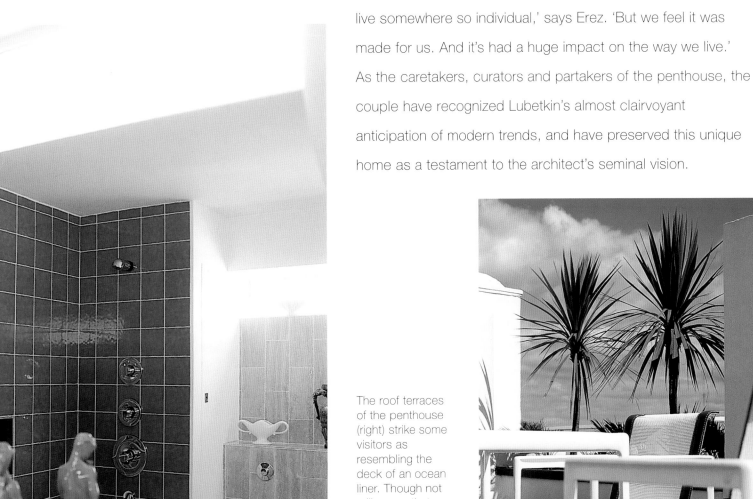

The roof terraces of the penthouse (right) strike some visitors as resembling the deck of an ocean liner. Though not a likeness that Lubetkin himself acknowledged, their sheer height and scale – and their openness to the elements – inspire a similar feeling of liberty and luxury.

curvy
colour

Hot colours,
sexy shapes
and wild,
surrealist
furniture in
a funky
Leeds loft

Mac MacLean is not afraid to break the rules. An exuberant estate agent turned developer, he has imprinted his playful ebullience on the interior of his show apartment and home in Simpsons Fold, the former textile factory that he has transformed into a flagship warehouse development in Leeds.

Having travelled to Canada and the USA to gather ideas and seek inspiration, Mac returned with the intention of finding a building in the heart of his home city that could bring New York-style loft living to Yorkshire.

A Historic Building   The factory building that attracted his attention had been derelict for about fifteen years but, sited in Dock Street and close to the waterfront on the River Aire, had fantastic potential for conversion. Parts of the Grade II-listed building date back to 1520, so expanses of beautiful original brickwork were revealed when plaster was stripped back, and there were 200-year-old beams and trusses still in excellent condition. The original Georgian windows were used as a template for replacement windows made from timber salvaged from the building, and, as far as possible, original features were restored and revealed.

The floor plan of MacLean's loft (right) is unashamedly post-modern, the snaking entrance hall opening up into the enormous living area.

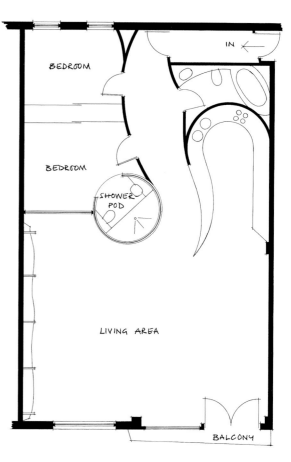

An architect's drawing (above) and also a computer-generated image (right) show how contrasts of old and new characterize this development, with its shining glazed penthouse surmounting the old brick of the former factory.

The six-storey building will accommodate ground-floor retail space and twenty-seven apartments, including a breathtaking 600m² steel and glass penthouse with ceilings over 10m high, which surmounts the building like 'the tiara on a duchess', as one Leeds paper observed. With solar-powered heating, its own lift, gymnasium, rooftop running track and restaurant-style kitchen, this million-pound loft is symbolic of the confidence of MacLean and his architect Gordon Carey (of Carey Jones Architects), and the sense of fun that they have brought to the whole development.

Throughout the apartment, one is immediately struck by the absence of right angles. Everything flows and bends so that, to the unaccustomed eye, it seems peculiarly energetic – almost alive.

Flexibility Their principal objective was to create exciting, flexible spaces. Some of the units were sold as shells, but in the others Gordon has designed interior walls that can be unscrewed and repositioned so as to alter the layout of the space or, if necessary, to create an extra bedroom. The lofts also feature 'islands' in the living areas that may be used as bars or workstations.

An S-shaped Space

Mac's own apartment, which is also the show loft, deftly demonstrates Carey's light touch. He has been involved in the conversion of a number of listed buildings, and it would seem that working within the constraints of conservation is a stimulus to his imagination. Designed in a huge S shape, which is described by the ceiling profiling, the curving and transparent walls of Mac's loft maximize the effect of light and space. The kitchen wraps around one end of the apartment, and there is a circular shower, constructed of glass blocks, in the centre. As Malcolm Cross, the project manager and planning supervisor, observes, 'The open-plan environment gives almost unlimited flexibility of use.' The partitioning that creates the bedrooms and bathroom, for example, has been designed to be removable should a future tenant want to enlarge the living area.

Designed in a great S-shaped sweep, the open-plan kitchen, hall and living areas are unified by a vigorous and rhythmical interplay of bright colour and fluid form.

Homely Hedonism This sinuous, open-plan interior is designed for pleasure. Mac sees the lofts as being ideal for young professionals who, after a hard day at work, want to entertain, listen to music and relax. He says, 'We wanted to create a space that is a lot of fun . . . The hall is huge and it's definitely the place for grand greetings.'

Creative Colours Despite its resolute modernism, the atmosphere of this loft is very far from aloof. The sizzling colour scheme chosen by Mac and Gordon combines vivid orange, lime green and electric blue, making the light interior seem even brighter. 'When you've got a big loft space,' says Mac, 'you can get away with big, powerful colours.' The 3m-high ceiling is the only expanse of white in an otherwise polychromatic scheme, though the vibrant colours are also grounded by the mellow tones of the mahogany floor, salvaged from Kirkburton Primary, Mac's old school.

The loft is 18m from wall to wall, so every effort was made to make the most of the light flooding in the floor-to-ceiling windows, principally through the use of glass-block walls. Mac's belief that light is the most important element in a loft also led him to use glass doors and to separate the living room and bedroom with a semi-see-through polycarbonate wall.

Artificial Light   Over seventy light fittings in the apartment boost the natural light, allowing lighting effects to be very closely controlled. Most of these fittings are halogen downlighters that stud the ceiling like a sparkling necklace. But Mac has also introduced theatrical elements: the wall-mounted aluminium

In this loft every detail conforms to a surreal and playful look. The bookshelf resembles a cascade of coloured water and the 'sperm' lighting (right) wittily evokes the creation of new life.

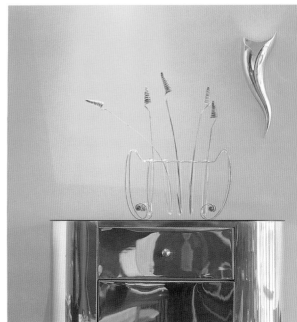

sperm light fittings (from MDW of London) that echo the sperm handles on the doors can be lit up at night to create an effect that Mac describes as being 'just like 1930s car headlights in the fog.'

Sensuous Shapes   The living area is characterized by sensuous, sinuous curves throughout. What Mac couldn't buy, he designed in tandem with Gordon Carey, so the unusual wavy buttress shelves that flow out of the wall like cascades of pure colour were made on site.

The furniture that Mac and his wife Pauline have chosen for the apartment is entirely in keeping with the bright and light-hearted look of this unit. A love of contemporary furniture led them to trawl international design exhibitions from which they have picked stylish, witty and

The hoofed furniture appears almost like animals grazing in a psychedelic landscape.

essentially practical pieces. The Miami Green leather-covered sofa and chairs (from Body To) combine comfort with modernity, the pointed chair back echoing the horned, demonic-looking dining chairs (from Chairs of London, a company well known for its outrageous designs). This is furniture with personality – it almost seems alive – as if the yellow and orange stools will run off on their aluminium legs and the kitsch piano stool (from By Design) metamorphose back into the zebra its fabric imitates. So witty and characterful are these pieces that one barely notices the Hofmann grand piano sitting discreetly in the bay created

by what is undoubtedly the most unusual feature of this loft – the circular shower that projects right out into the middle of the living area.

The Shower Pod This unusual juxtaposition is the ultimate demonstration of Mac's flamboyance. It was originally designed to be of Flemish translucent glass blocks from floor to ceiling, but when Gordon Carey suggested that this might make the views from the living area a little too spectacular, Mac allowed him to add the blue modesty panel. With a diameter of 2.5m, this good-sized room also accommodates a lavatory and a large stainless steel basin and still feels spacious. As a central feature, it makes a grand statement about luxury and the place of sensuous pleasure in the heart of the home: Mac describes the

Positioned right in the centre of the loft, this shower room (right), with its Tardis-like qualities, makes an up-front statement about the pleasures of water and exposure (it originally lacked the blue modesty panel).

The leopard-print fabric of this high-backed chair (below) is ostentatiously sexy and kitsch, but this is, equally, another animal in Mac's loft safari.

In both the shower pod (right) and the bathroom (below) marine-style details – most notably the small, functional-looking stainless steel sink and the porthole mirrors – give these watery oases a neat, nautical look.

gentle spray of the overhead shower, with its watering-can head, as being like 'bathing in Miami rain'. The whole shower pod resembles the funnel of a ship, and the marine metaphor is reiterated in the bathroom, where mirror portholes stud the walls and the same green and white tiling has been used.

A Convivial Kitchen Sited at one end of the open-plan living space, the kitchen area is defined by the great sweep of the Canadian maple breakfast bar, and boasts a glistening steel Amana American fridge-freezer, which, with its double doors and external ice maker, helps to create an hospitable atmosphere. The flanking clear-glass larders also contribute to a look that is open, clean and inviting, as does the stainless steel sink and gleaming, funnel-like extractor hood.

The Wardrobe Wall The two bedrooms are cleverly connected by a 3m-high bird's-eye maple double-sided wardrobe, which looks like a great wooden wall in each room. Here again, Mac has avoided the rectilinear: the edge of the sliding door is profiled into a series of fluid, naturalistic curves, and it has a metre-long chrome sperm handle that is set at a sweeping angle.

A notion of 'truth to materials' informs the contrast between shining steel appliances and bespoke wooden furnishings. In the kitchen (above) the blond wooden worktop describes a broad, organic curve. In the bedrooms the bird's-eye maple doors (right) are profiled to appear as if freshly cut from the tree.

Boldness and Brio A grand master of hyperbole, Mac has created a loft that exploits to the full the potential of the building – the high ceilings, huge windows interesting brickwork and original timber – while being an extravagant showcase for the avant garde. The loft is reached by a narrow, dark, almost Dickensian stairway, so that the impression on entering this light and vivid space is of emerging from a storm into a rainbow.

the top storey

Chic city style in a new but original warehouse home, once a repository for fine leathers

n 1852 the old Morocco Store building was erected as a warehouse for Moroccan leather, conveniently sited among tanneries and curriers only a street away from London's vast Bermondsey leather market.

This compact four-storey building is typical of Victorian industrial architecture, having a brick façade, wide, recessed windows separated by brick pilasters, and external doors at each storey that allowed goods to be admitted by winch. In the 1940s these doors disappeared when the building became a warehouse for Scottish Malt Products, but otherwise the change of function had little impact on the robust structure of the building.

Old and New   When Andrew Wadsworth of Landworth Properties (part of The Waterhouse Group) alighted on the Morocco Store as a potential site for development, he was struck by the possibility of restoring the architectural features, including the loading doors, to re-establish the proper proportions of the original design. A small, adjacent two-storey Victorian building had been destroyed by bombing during the war, and in this space he envisaged a new block based on the architecture of nearby warehouses and following the design of the original building.

Unusual Timber   So interested was Andrew in the maintaining the integrity of the original Victorian design and materials that he decided the new building should have a wooden structure. African greenheart timber was much used by the Victorians for its permanence and solidity.

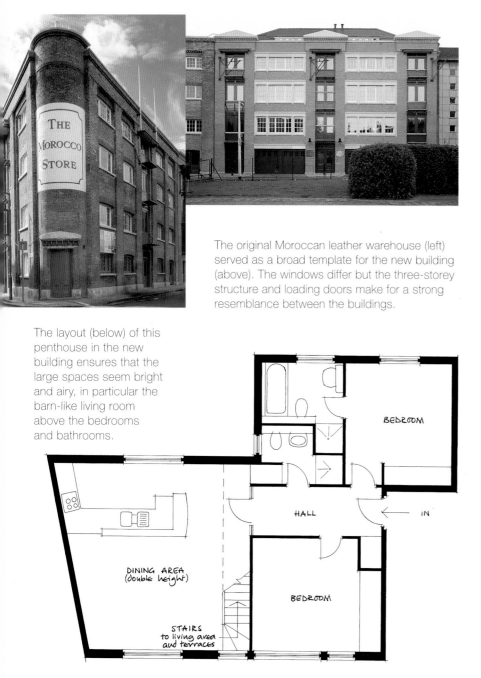

The original Moroccan leather warehouse (left) served as a broad template for the new building (above). The windows differ but the three-storey structure and loading doors make for a strong resemblance between the buildings.

The layout (below) of this penthouse in the new building ensures that the large spaces seem bright and airy, in particular the barn-like living room above the bedrooms and bathrooms.

BEDROOM

HALL   ← IN

DINING AREA
(double height)

BEDROOM

STAIRS
to living area
and terraces

This apartment boasts spectacular views, both within and without. Looking down from the top of the stairs, it is possible to take in the entire width of the lower level from front to back. The far wall is part of the original building.

So heavy that it doesn't float and denser than brick, it was favoured for the construction of jetties (as it is also relatively impervious to water). This astonishing wood, which grows fairly quickly, is now available from sustainable sources, and so seemed an appropriately natural but heavy-duty material for the new extension. The new Morocco Store is the first modern building in which this wood has been used, but as greenheart timber also needs no fire-proofing and can easily support concrete floors, a structural wooden frame seemed both a practical and an historically apt choice.

Brick and Stone   The chosen brick was new London yellow stock, which, though brighter than the original brick, blends well with it, particularly as the architect, Jonathan Dransfield, has been careful to echo the detailing of the old building in the full-height pilasters and dentil decoration above the upper storey.

The most notable difference between the two buildings is in the shape and design of the windows, which are larger and more classical in the extension, with stone casements making for a stronger horizontal emphasis. This adaptation provides the new apartments with the greatest amount of available light and has the effect of brightening the façade, giving it a fresh, more contemporary appearance.

This felicitous combination of the old and the new is characteristic of Landworth's objectives in the development as a whole. Landworth Properties is known principally for its loft developments – all but two of the other apartments in the Morocco Store have been sold as shells – so this penthouse loft has been a playground for Andrew's imagination, allowing him to realize his own vision of the perfect loft interior (see also High Drama, pages 140–9).

The penthouse is situated on the top floor of the new block but shares a wall with the old building. In the kitchen/dining area the party wall is therefore of original Victorian brick and the gable walls of new London yellow stock. In keeping with this juxtaposition, the interior fittings and furnishings are appropriately eclectic. The timber beams give the space a barn-like quality; a marble Corinthian column serves as a plant stand; and the kitchen is of a high specification, with every modern convenience but finished in a fresh smalt blue that lends it something of the atmosphere of a French country house.

The Theatre of the Interior   The effect is comfortable and inviting, but in a way that is far from bland. Having created a space that – with its double-height pitched timber ceiling – is intensely dramatic, Andrew has introduced strong textures and colours that give the area a warm and sumptuous atmosphere.

From a moderately sized hallway (left) one enters the tall, broad space that is the hub of the apartment (below), accommodating – but without crowding – kitchen, dining and study zones.

Cooking and Dining   The modernist zinc-panelled exterior of the kitchen is in appealing contrast with the rich wood tones of a distinctive triangular tallboy – a Thai antique. This space is clearly not the result of a theoretical interior design, worked out on paper and then bought wholesale, but of the personal by-eye judgements that make for a characterful home.

The kitchen/dining area has been carefully lit for a warm and intimate effect. Sparkling 12-volt halogen fittings are suspended over the kitchen surfaces on stainless steel wires, and a free-standing torpedo-shaped lamp sheds a warm glow over the mellow tones of the oak floorboards. A discreet task light over the glass-topped trestle desk provides further soft illumination.

Fine Details   A distinctive feature of this loft are the unusual galvanized steel doors, which – perhaps surprisingly – seem totally compatible with the natural textures and hues of the wood and brick. Their unashamed modernism is accentuated between the hall and the kitchen by a glass-block frame to the doorway, which is both practical (allowing light into the hall) and chic. Again, in the hallway itself, a Thai antique – an oak side table – immediately establishes a welcoming and homely atmosphere.

Comfort and Texture   Andrew has used exposed plaster for the hall and bedroom walls, which, with its warm tones and attractive patina, again both complements and artfully contradicts the industrial modernism of the steel and glass. The steel door frames look almost as if they were pushed into soft clay walls – to sculptural effect.

The two bedrooms in this apartment are of average size, but seem roomy by virtue of their unfussy design and furnishings: ribbed, coir-like wool carpet; galvanized bed bases; canvas wardrobes; and natural coloured linen curtains on metal poles.

Attention to Detail   The apartment also has two immaculately finished bathrooms, the details of which were planned in 1:1 scale drawings so as to ensure that there would be no cut tiles. Here the lines and surfaces are clean and restrained and the colours muted, but warm and earth-toned. The effect is modern and functional, yet the mood relaxing – concealed downlighters are also gentle on the eyes. Zinc, green Cumberland slate and prime American oak create an interplay of texture that gives the room far more personality than most bathrooms in fitted-out lofts.

The Barn Room   Andrew describes this loft as 'a converted barn in the city', and at the upper level this is exactly how it appears. On ascending the plain timber staircase one enters a large,

Raw plaster (above) is an unusual finish that blends well with the exposed brickwork of the bedrooms' exterior walls.

In warm colours and with baffled lighting, the bathroom (below) offers a private retreat from the social spaces of the loft.

open living area that is indeed barn-like with its 6m-high pitched timber roof, oak floor, plaster walls and unusual wood-burning stove. But Andrew doesn't allow the country idiom – however attractive – to become pastiche. His eclectic aesthetic permits Le Corbusier's famous Grand Confort leather chairs and a Viaduct sofa to bring a sophisticated urban glamour to the interior, an effect reinforced by other carefully chosen modern designs: Conran Shop light fittings, an Eileen Gray table, and a Habitat wool rug in abstract blues and greens.

The barn-like upper storey could feel cold and inhospitable, but with its unusual wood-burning stove, exposed beams and the soft, enveloping furniture, it has the comfortable atmosphere of a country cottage. The night brings spectacular views of floodlit Tower Bridge (right).

Outdoor Rooms with a View

A special feature of this distinctive living room is its two large terraces to north and south that offer the attractions of *al fresco* dining and container gardening. At the architectural plans stage Andrew was aware that these terraces would significantly extend the living space in summer. But what he could not predict (without going up in a cherry-picker) was just how spectacular would be the city skyline to the north, with Tower Bridge clearly visible, stunningly floodlit at night.

off beam

A great barn of a place – the reclamation and restoration of an eighteenth-century hayloft

As a property developer principally involved with the refurbishment of historic buildings, William Broadbent is appalled by most barn conversions. In his view, turning working barns into suburban-style homes – often complete with latticed windows – represents the desecration of some of the most interesting traditional buildings in England. Accordingly, his conversion of an eighteenth-century oak-and-flint hayloft and cow shed in the English Sussex downs looks like a barn rather than an executive residence.

Developing Taste   Born in the famous old Thames-side pub, The Prospect of Whitby, William was surrounded from the

A floor plan (right) clearly shows the connection between the hayloft and barn and demonstrates the impressive size of the sitting room. Only over the bedrooms has a second floor been inserted; elsewhere is clear space between ground and beams.

The enormous external shutters (above) appear original but are in fact replicas, recreated in exact detail, down to the very method of construction.

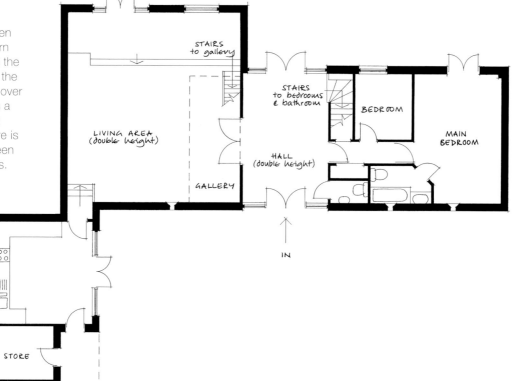

STAIRS to gallery

STAIRS to bedrooms & bathroom

BEDROOM

LIVING AREA (double height)

MAIN BEDROOM

HALL (double height)

GALLERY

IN

STORE

first by traditional architecture and by antiques – his grandfather was a passionate connoisseur with a particular interest in clocks. These early influences have clearly shaped his taste, and he has gathered an impressive collection of horological and nautical antiques and scientific instruments of all sorts. A telescope mounted on a tripod in the sitting room is one of many objects that give the space the feel of an observatory or of a scientist's study. These instruments are objects of great beauty, but they are also functional, a balance that is a key aesthetic of William's distinctive interior.

Traditional Methods and Materials   In the conversion of this barn, William's innate feel for the beauty of things industrial has led him to try to retain the integrity of the

original space. He was attracted to the building by the silver grey colour of its oak frame and the satisfying texture of its rough flint walls, and these basic structural materials have been repaired but are otherwise unmodified. In fact, this conversion is more aptly termed a restoration because, where new elements have been introduced, Willliam has either modelled them exactly on the originals or reconstructed them of sympathetic materials reclaimed from appropriate sources. The enormous external shutters are exact replicas of the original ones that had rotted beyond repair. And no concessions have been made to their residential use: two men are still required to move them. As William observes, 'There is nothing domestic or residential about the exterior.' And it is certainly true that the exterior of the building still looks like a country barn.

Where new oak beams were introduced – lifted in by crane – these were left untreated so as to age and mellow in tone naturally, eventually to become a similar hue to the original timber. William was also keen that original construction methods should be used, so the workmen – a team of hand-picked local craftsman – fashioned oak pegs in the traditional manner.

As the enormous roof was beyond repair, William thought he would have no choice but to buy a new roofing material, but, by happy chance, his craftsmen were able to purchase 17,000 roof tiles from a 175-year-old brewery in Kent. With their rich red hue and attractive weathered patina, these look entirely original, blending perfectly with the deep, subtle tones of the shutters and decorative brickwork.

This barn is not so much a conversion as a restoration, every effort having been made to use reclaimed and like materials in sympathetic ways and to leave original features, like the windslips (above), unmodified and intact.

Antiques, scientific
instruments and
nautical collectables
populate the awe-
inspiring, triple-height
sitting room (opposite).
The rich but orderly
profusion of these
objects seems perfectly
fitting within the rustic
embrace of the
weathered oak beams –
a barn is essentially a
storehouse.

Open Space   Such sensitivity is equally apparent in the interior, which, with its enormous glazed hall and soaring, triple-height sitting room, retains hayloft dimensions. In these important areas of the barn, William has avoided segmenting and carving up the space, and, as far as possible, has limited structural interventions. A new wooden gallery creates a mezzanine study above the sitting area, but otherwise oak posts and beams are the only elements that divide the living area.

From Vision to Reality   William didn't enlist services of a large architectural practice to design the interior layout. Rather, he engaged a local architectural draughtsman to help realize his own vision of a lofty barn home. After looking at many books on traditional rural buildings, together they arrived at a plan that capitalized on the grand scale of the

space but also provided smaller, more intimate areas for the sake of comfort, warmth and practicality. These differences of scale, so consummately achieved, give Burgh Barn the duel benefits of a loft and a cottage – monumental and inspirational, but, equally, homely and habitable.

Fine Detail   Such sensitive conversion has earned the building a Grade II listing, and each room of the barn displays the attention to detail that one might expect in the restoration of an important historic building. The hall is defined exactly by the width of the original shuttered opening and its height is uninterrupted, so that the same central 'gap' remains the visual focus from

As well as providing a
convenient study area,
the new sitting room
gallery (above) creates
a deep doorway
between sitting room
and hall that makes the
passage from one
grand space to another
all the more impressive.

the exterior. At ground level the floorboards are of pitch pine – like the roof tiles, reclaimed from an old property, in this case an early nineteenth-century house in Brighton. The only modification made by William's craftsmen was to kiln-dry them to avoid their moving over time. A number of the doors were also constructed of these floorboards, made on site by a local carpenter. Even the ironwork on these doors was especially made to a 300-year-old design, and the Norfolk-style locks have latches of real leather.

The Menagerie   Just as the barn has, in William's hands, become a beautifully preserved historic building, so it seems that its original animal inhabitants have made the transition from life to art. Appropriately, a full-sized animal stands in the hall; not a cow or a sheep, but a zebra that looks as if it has just run in from the garden. This fine wooden sculpture, which William bought directly from the artist Nick Johnson, is the chief representative of another leitmotif in William's collection: antique and wooden animals. His menagerie includes a Victorian stuffed Emperor penguin, a stuffed barn owl (which sits with alarming realism on the newel post in the hall), a wooden cockerel, and a large goose, also by Nick Johnson. The effect is witty, somewhat surreal, and enormously vivid, the animals enlivening the space and providing an appealing counterpoint to the scientific instruments.

The wide, open plain of the hall is, by implication, large enough for a zebra to run in. The sculptor Nick Johnson's stunning full-size centrepiece serves to emphasize the scale of the barn's central hall.

The enormous sitting room is well filled with furniture, objects and pictures, yet the basic symmetry of the furnishings lends a degree of formality fitting to the grandeur of the space.

Simple Style The decoration and furnishing of the hall is restrained and unostentatious. A traditional Orkney chair, made of wood and string, provides a frugal seat, and the restrained stairway, discreetly recessed into the wall, is of the simplest construction, without decorative detailing of any kind. Its aesthetic is more hayloft than home, William here demonstrating once again his distaste for decorative anachronisms. The open-beamed roof of the hall immediately establishes the lofty look of the interior, and serves as a visual preface to the stunning oak-beamed construction of the sitting room.

Light and Heat   The conversion and restoration of this space, the principal room, provided William and his craftsmen with their single greatest challenge. Underpinning was required and an enormous quantity of concrete needed to make the floor level. William's firm belief that barns need not be dark led him to make the provision of natural light the first priority of his design. Accordingly, the 10m-high space is left as open as possible, a small 3m-high oak gallery (used as a study area) providing the only mezzanine intervention. Above this gallery the entire wall between the hall and the sitting room is glazed, an unusual but visually unobtrusive means of flooding light on to the mezzanine and into the roof spaces.

Typical of William Broadbent's inspired acquisitions, this mid nineteenth-century Guyanese carving of a canoe (right) has figures individually dressed in monkey skins.

In the hall a scale model of a Tigermoth (below right) draws the eye up to the full height of the beams.

The Punch heads (above) are fairground cast-offs. William Broadbent collects painted wooden objects from all countries and periods, but 'only if dilapidated enough', with the paintwork appealingly distressed (not unlike the weathered beams of the barn itself).

The light level is further boosted by a square roof-light that, needless to say, is not a standard Velux window, but a metal English Heritage-designed reproduction of an antique black lead factory roof window. Even the original windslips, that provided ventilation to dry the hay, have been turned into opening windows and a wall of 3m-high double-glazed windows in semi-hardwood frames pours light into the lower level of the room. This huge space therefore seems airy and bright throughout – and far from cold. High-tech roof insulation ensures that the warmth of the sunlight is trapped and, in winter, an industrial, wood-burning stove in the centre of the room – new, but based on a Heath Robinsonesque nineteenth-century design – gives out enough heat to warm the entire barn.

Objects of Desire   Given the size of the sitting room and the purity of its decoration (simply whitewashed throughout), it can house William's eclectic treasures – antique furniture, textiles, rugs, paintings, prints, instruments, models and curios – without seeming cluttered or visually overwhelming. Sitting in one of the early nineteenth-century English armchairs, you can take in an enormous Victorian cupboard, the black paint of which has distressed to a satisfying crazed texture. Above this hangs a very rare eighteenth-century Chinese scroll painting of a family tree, and before it is a modern sofa to which antique kelim cushions lend distinction. William is particularly keen on eighteenth- and nineteenth-century English country stick furniture, a perfect example of which – a primitive Shaker-looking chair – sits on a vivid antique Sumak rug. Boat-maker's models, a telescope trained on the sky, ship's ropes hanging from the beams and a 5m anaconda skin displayed on the wall all contribute to the inspired mixed message of this interior – at once a barn, a ship and a museum, but above all a comfortable and welcoming home.

This inspired combination of intimacy and grandeur sets the tone for the rest of the house. The whitewashed freshness is a tabula rasa for the many treasures that William has combined with an artistic eye backed by a connoisseur's

The strong vertical thrust of the dark beams means that even the smaller rooms, such as the study, seem tall and airy, able to accommodate such substantial objects as this nineteenth-century American roll-top desk.

knowledge. Despite the self-imposed orthodoxy of William's barn restoration, there are no rules when it comes to the objects he is happy to house together: a one-third-scale model of a Tigermoth flying in the hall; a nineteenth-century American roll-top walnut desk in the upstairs study; new prints of Italian villas in the sitting room; fairground models of Punch in the guest bedroom; and a nineteenth-century Guyanese carving of a canoe with figures clad in monkey skin that presides over the bedhead of the principal bedroom.

The high-quality look of the kitchen was, in fact, achieved at minimal expense, the units being designed and constructed by William's carpenters out of wooden planks.

A Unifying Vision

That these diverse objects from around the world sit so comfortably together is a testament to the clarity of William's vision in designing the interior of Burgh Barn. The homogeneity of his decorative approach – Spartan walls and floors serving as exhibition spaces for objects of particular beauty – give the entire space a satisfying coherence, the smaller bedrooms and study seeming to partake of the same airiness and openness as the hall and sitting room.

The Creative Challenge

When William bought the barn, its lack of everything – from a suitable roof to exterior shutters – may have seemed a distinct disadvantage. In fact, starting from scratch (the building also lacked every basic utility) with a moderate budget and little time (only twenty-six weeks from start to finish) fostered an inventive and focused approach. As the craftsmen became more familiar with William's needs and taste, they made suggestions that were both

The simplicity and restraint, muted colours and natural textures of Burgh Barn extends to the landscape architecture, which is unforced and unfussy.

cost-saving and aesthetically satisfying. The African slate of the kitchen floor, for example, wasn't exorbitantly priced and provided the warm colour and rich texture more often found in a reclaimed stone floor. The units, too, were simply constructed on site out of wooden planks, and finished in a standard commercial cream paint. It is in just such touches that the close relationship between William and his craftsmen has borne fruit. Although he appointed an on-site project manager to oversee the restoration and refurbishment, he was himself present at weekend site meetings, there to advise and guide his highly motivated team. This hands-on approach was particularly beneficial when, for instance, the lighting was being finalized. William favoured low-voltage lighting throughout – important for the preservation of light-sensitive objects – and was on hand to make critical decisions about how his treasures should best be lit.

It is now only three years since William bought the barn and surrounding land, but today even the garden looks as though it has never been otherwise than established. Although twenty tonnes of topsoil and vast quantities of drought-resistant plants had to be imported to the site, the effect, like the house, is unostentatious, a simple oval pool providing the calming equivalent of the whitewashed walls within.

From
classroom to
class home,
an architect
who walks
his talk in
South London

cool school

Victorian school architecture is distinguished by its grand scale, sound construction, fine brickwork and interesting architectural ornament. This is true of the enormous London Board school, the Tabard, that houses the apartments featured on pages 82–101, but is equally the case in the far smaller 1870s Dulwich schoolhouse that the architectural practice of Brookes Stacey Randall has sensitively converted into a highly unusual London home for partner Nik Randall.

Opening Up   When Nik and the textile designer Suzsi Corio bought the school, it basically consisted of a long, rectangular space subdivided into two classrooms with low, suspended ceilings. Given the generous floor area of 120m², Brookes Stacey Randall's first objective was to maintain the feeling of spaciousness while, at the same time, providing the largest possible amount of flexible accommodation.

The removal of the suspended ceiling more than doubled the vertical height to a grand 7.5m and revealed sturdy but graceful overarching oak beams. When the dividing wall was also removed, the resulting great hall was so impressive that Nik was loath to cut into it with mezzanine floors. However, as these were vital to provide the accommodation and flexibility needed, Nik and the project architect, Daniel Bérubé, decided to 'hang' the principal, solid mezzanine in mid-air, an effect achieved by the insertion of glazed strips along its sides. In practice, this means that from ground level one can see up to the apex of the roof and, equally, sunlight can shine down to the lower floor. Accordingly, the mezzanine, which supports bedroom areas and a bathroom, seems neither weighty nor over-large.

Clear Contrasts   Brookes Stacey Randall's respect for the original fabric of the building is particularly apparent in the way they have treated the walls. That the white wall

opposite
Unimpeded by the glass-floored mezzanine, sunshine floods in through the original windows and the new skylights, to illuminate the sitting area.

A plan of the converted school (right) shows how the flexible study/playroom/dining space can be completely closed off by a fourth 'wall' of sliding screens. The mezzanines at either end of the building allow a vast floor-to-ceiling void over the principal living area.

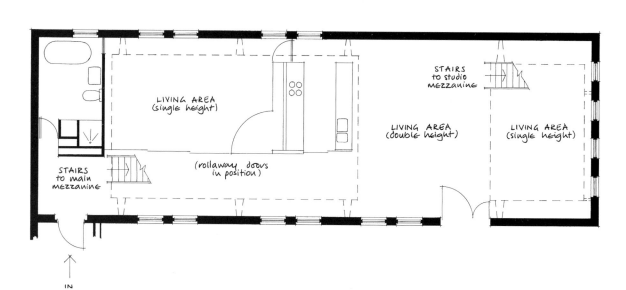

LIVING AREA
(single height)

STAIRS
to studio
mezzanine

LIVING AREA
(double height)

LIVING AREA
(single height)

STAIRS
to main
mezzanine

(rollaway doors in position)

IN

Because of the ingenious suspension of the main mezzanine and its glazed strip edges (above), the hallway seems particularly open and very airy, with a view up the full height of the exterior wall.

lining, which conveniently houses the cabling and pipework, is not the original wall surface is made clear by its stopping short of the stone quoins, thereby revealing some of the original brickwork in the resulting recess. Here old and new combine, not in a fudged confusion – the old made to look new and the new old – but clearly juxtaposed and contrasted, the original building being the matrix for a new, flexible and quintessentially modern home, the aim being, as Nik puts it, 'to touch the original fabric of the building very lightly and to complement its appearance.'

The Yellow Wall   On entering the apartment – reached up an original Victorian stone staircase – one is immediately struck by an enormous expanse of colour: a bright yellow wall that stands like a tall, sculptural object stretching the full height of the old school. Like the mezzanines, it is separated from the outer wall by wide strips of glass (in this case etched glass for the sake of privacy in the bathroom), which emphasizes the effect of a free-standing monolith rather than a dividing wall. As Nik explains, 'You see the envelope of the building passing around the block of the yellow wall, and the strong colour draws the eye up into the roof space.'

Open-tread stairs rising up beside the yellow wall have mesh side panels (right), which contribute to the apparent lightness and don't obstruct the sense of space.

With the rolling doors retracted, even the floor lines are clear of interruptions, the desk/filing cabinet unit (below) suspended so that it provides a discrete visual element against the wall.

Flexible Usage   On the other side of this wall is a large, open, relatively bare area. A grey lacquered desk and filing cabinet unit, wall mounted so as not to interrupt the line of the floor – faces a row of similarly lacquered full-height cupboard doors. A few toys are visible, but the use of this 'room' is not immediately apparent. When asked, Nik observes that 'there are no rooms as such, but areas that can serve different functions.' Here purpose-designed storage and sliding screens allow the space to be an office, playroom, guest bedroom or dining room. When pulled out from the yellow wall, three sliding screens create a fourth wall that closes off the room from the corridor space. The right-hand cupboard door then opens back to shut the room off entirely. Currently, the area is principally used as a playroom – large enough to pitch a tent in, as Nik has sometimes done to entertain Louis – but its flexible use means that, when he is older and wants a private space, a teenager's den is ready and waiting for him. Not only is Nik's home a converted space, but it is itself simply convertible into the spaces that may be required in the future. As Nik points out, one of the key aspects of Brookes Stacey Randall's design is that the 'furniture' works hard to meet practical needs. The mezzanine balustrades offer a further example of this aesthetic pragmatism, one doubling as a bookshelf and the other as a workbench.

The Cinema Kitchen   Sited in the centre of the space – the heart of the home – is the kitchen, which can be both an open-plan cook station and an enclosed galley according to need. Built into a wall of units, the main cooking area can be completely concealed by the simple action of lowering a pair of up-and-over doors, and sliding screens which close to one side of the free-standing unit, turning it into a separate room. Finally, a 3.6m-long blind can be lowered to create a third 'wall' adjacent to the main living space. In practice, this is rarely used, but has come in very handy on occasions when the kitchen has been piled with dishes and visitors have turned up unexpectedly. True to the spirit of inventiveness at Brookes Stacey Randall, this device doubles as a projection screen, transforming the living area into a mini cinema.

When the up-and-over doors of the kitchen are closed it appears hardly to be a kitchen at all, and can indeed be entirely concealed behind the roll-down projection screen – just visible in the upper part of the picture. With the doors open, the kitchen looks not unlike a market stall.

Possibly the most spectacular feature of this school conversion is the glazed mezzanine, which effectively allows the void over the principal living area to extend to the gable end. Suzsi Corio laughs that the workmen were afraid to stand on it, despite being prepared to clamber about on the scaffolding outside.

The cool grey-green lacquer of the units makes this kitchen seem calm and recessive. Its low key colour scheme is very far from the brash looks of what may be termed 'shiny metal modernism' – which would be totally out of keeping with the subtle, natural tones of this building's original materials.

The Glass Mezzanine At the other end of the space a second mezzanine platform also appears suspended as if by magic. Here the architectural solution to keeping the hall light and whole is even more radical and exciting. A studio for Suzsi's textile design business, Corio Studio, its floor is glazed with thick clear glass, so that it appears like an open iron frame rather than as a dividing and enclosing solid platform. Sunshine pours through the roof-light into the studio and down – unimpeded – to the living area below. Indeed, this highly unusual solution allows Louis, Nik and Suzsi's three-year-old son, to lie on the sofa and look up through the floor at clouds and passing aeroplanes.

Open Intimacy Occupying more than a third of the ground level to one end of the school, the living area beneath the glass mezzanine benefits both from an entire wall of original windows at the gable end and from the light flooding down through the clear glass 'ceiling'. The partially enclosed nature of the space makes it feel warm and intimate, and a sofa, reclining chair and the long wall-mounted unit housing the television, hi-fi, etc., are all that is needed for comfort in an intrinsically relaxing space.

Moving Skywards The two mezzanines constitute the middle level of this extraordinary home. The solid mezzanine – with its sleeping and dressing areas – occupies one end of the school; the glass mezzanine the other, offering ample room both for machines and office equipment. These mezzanines are reached by graceful iron-and-wood staircases that – with their open, birch-ply treads – don't interrupt the spatial flow of the hall or living areas. A further staircase – made completely of glass to block the light as little as possible – rises from the studio mezzanine to the roof terrace, which, though relatively small, commands impressive views of the Barbican, Canary Wharf and, on a clear day, St Paul's Cathedral. Nik comments that, 'This increasing lightness [on walking up the stairs], from stone, to wood, to glass, accentuates the sense of rising from terra firma towards the sky.'

The sitting 'room' under the glass mezzanine lies behind the almost sculptural spine of another open-tread staircase. In most homes the under-stair area is only fit to house brooms; here, the stair's angle is used to dramatic effect to help create a specific zone.

Controllable Lights Just as the interior spaces have been organized for maximum flexibility of use, so the lighting design invites exciting transformations. The complete interior can be evenly lit to maintain the long views and emphasize the openness of the building, but, alternatively, individual, dimmable lights can be used at night to close the space down to smaller, more intimate areas.

The view from the glass studio mezzanine demonstrates how the volume of the shell has been kept as whole, intact and undivided as possible – to stunning effect.

Room for Expansion   Most intimate of all are the 'rooms' on the third level of the interior. Tucked under the roof of the principal mezzanine, each with a raised bed area, they can be used as additional bedrooms, dens or simply for storage. But, again, they offer Nik and Suzsi flexibility now and the reassurance of being able to meet future needs.

Together, these three levels increase the available floor area to 250m², without in any way interrupting the sense of the scale of the original building. If anything, the mezzanine levels make the void over the kitchen and dining areas appear all the more breathtaking.

Nik and his family use every part of the new layout, and he sees the main benefit of the design being that it allows area functions to be changed without one 'feeling that one is always on the edge of something else.' Too often this is a problem in loft spaces that are open-plan but otherwise unplanned.

baroque
bravado

Carved and gilded, painted and polished, a Victorian schoolroom transformed into a flamboyant seventeenth-century palace

A specialist in the design of historic interiors, Caroline Haelterman was renting a two-bedroom flat in London's Hyde Park Crescent, when, driving along the motorway, she saw an advertisement for 'Real Lofts'. The imminent sale of her flat, which she thought too overpriced to consider buying, was focusing her thoughts on the possibility of finding a property that offered greater value of money and wider scope for an unusual and highly personal interior design.

Recognizing Potential Despite whitewashed walls, seagrass floors and minimal decoration, the three huge rooms of the show flat of the Tabard – a converted Victorian London Board school building south of London Bridge – offered sufficient potential

for a full-blown Baroque treatment to make the property highly attractive to Caroline: 'I kept coming back to see it, realized I'd pay a million for this space in the centre of town and thought, let's do it.'

Recycling Schools Sapcote Real Lofts, developer of the Tabard, specializes in the conversion of period buildings for residential use. Since the 1960s it has won several conservation awards for the sympathetic re-use of buildings of architectural and historic interest, including convents, bakeries and – over the last ten years – a number of large Victorian schools in South London.

The grand proportions of these sound buildings, and their impressive architectural features – soaring ceilings, craftsman-built beams, enormous windows, attractive brickwork and fine detailing – make them ideal sites for conversion into lofts, an additional bonus being the former playground. The smallest loft spaces available in these school buildings are of around 100m², hence the emphasis on Real in the Sapcote company name. These apartments are truly lofty: the shells are sold with the ceiling heights unmodified, the original spaces largely undivided, and often the company creates fewer units than permitted in order to ensure that the ground plan of each loft is as satisfying and adaptable as possible. So sensitive and inventive has been the conversion of the Tabard (into fifteen loft apartments and one house) that the building has been Grade II listed.

London Board Schools tended to be finely constructed, often with distinctive architectural features such as the 'bell tower' in The Tabard (above). This school building now contains 15 loft apartments, including Caroine Haelterman's and the contrasting De Metz Green conversion (see pages 93–101).

Viewed from the mezzanine (above), the grandeur of the décor seems perfectly in keeping with the scale of the original schoolroom space. The reclaimed strapwork door surrounds are particularly effective in making the new door opening (to the bedroom) appear in proportion with the sand-blasted wall.

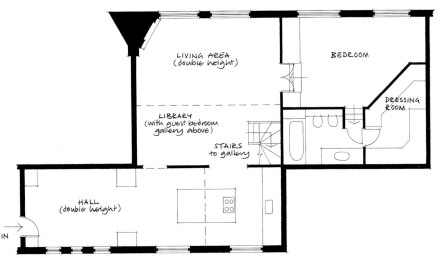

LIVING AREA
(double height)

BEDROOM

LIBRARY
(with guest bedroom
gallery above)

DRESSING
ROOM

STAIRS
to gallery

HALL
(double height)

IN

The original shell consisted of three large room spaces that can be clearly seen on the plan (left). The neat mezzanine level straddling parts of the kitchen and living room has been carefully handled in the context of the style of the apartment, and designed to look more like a gallery than a platform.

Victorian Virtues Sapcote has completely renovated the school, its intention being 'to display to its best the existing Victorian architecture without detracting from the original aesthetic of light, space and good air circulation, while introducing the benefits of modern technology in keeping with today's individual live/work requirements and expectations.' Or, as Sapcote's literature states, 'I've always thought lofty meant tall. How come then so many people have been merrily whistling "height ho" on their way to buying lofts of Danny de Vito proportions?'

Externally, parking spaces were created within a secure compound and an attractive garden was landscaped. Internally, fire and soundproofing was carried out and the services – plumbing, gas, electricity and a phone line – brought to the front door of each unit. When Caroline first saw her new home, it consisted of three enormous whitewashed rooms connected by original doorways, effectively a blank canvas for the exercise of her astonishing visual imagination and professional expertise. The only constraint was Sapcote's total ban on Austrian blinds and net curtains – a restriction not likely to stifle creativity. As a heading in Sapcote's promotional literature pithily observes, 'Alice Bands Don't Live Here Any More', and the resident profile is certainly not characterized by lovers of frou-frou window treatments.

Going Over the Top Loft living is all about breaking with norms but, like any new movement, it has developed orthodoxies of its own: clean lines, hard floors, minimal decoration, classic modern furniture, and – of course – high-tech appliances. This may be an appropriate aesthetic for a converted space, but it is one that Caroline Haelterman has had no qualms in subverting in the creation of her extraordinary apartment.

Classic 'before and after' shots reveal just how far Caroline has been prepared to go in transforming the minimal shell (left) into an intensely flamboyant Baroque interior. Such a wholehearted flouting of a modernist aesthetic is very unusual in a contemporary loft.

The sale went through in 1997 and since then Caroline has been working ceaselessly to transform her three-room space into a Baroque palace. By introducing a mezzanine floor, she has increased the living area to a very commodious 200m², so that she now has a living room of 6m wide and long and 9m high, two bedrooms, two bathrooms, a dressing room and a long entrance hall-cum-office-cum-kitchen, more than ample accommodation for Caroline and her Russian Blue cat, Cyrano, even filled as it is with monumental seventeenth-century treasures. 'My father says it looks like a brothel in here, but I love it. Louis XIV is my idol, and the whole theme of the flat is the seventeenth century – the early stuff, not the frilly bits you see at Versailles. I couldn't live with concrete, glass and steel: I respect minimalism, but it's not for me.'

Freed from the constraint of designing for others, Caroline wanted to put her personal stamp on this apartment, and therefore aimed for what she acknowledges is an over-the-top Baroque treatment more readily associated with grand properties, such as the French château Vaux le Vicomte that provided her main inspiration. She specifically wanted to avoid any run of the mill design options, and so was her own architect, interior designer and, to a large extent, decorator. Caroline has therefore been responsible for every detail of this wonderfully eccentric interior – from the mock rustication of the hall to the choice of hangings on the seventeenth-century four-poster bed.

Back to Basics   It might be thought that in dissenting from a modernist aesthetic Caroline has had to work against the ethos of a modern converted shell

apartment, but in practice the basic elements of the Tabard show flat have been just as amenable to this historic treatment as to modern interpretation (see pages 93–101). The walls were sand-blasted to remove every trace of white paint – 'Too cold in tone for the style I wanted' – revealing yellow London-stock brick that has a rich, varied texture, a warm hue and even some decorative detailing – the stripes of red brickwork are a typically Victorian trait. This done, Caroline vacuumed and sealed every single brick.

Having discussed her ideas with her ex-associate Douglas Adams, she also made a few significant structural changes that entirely transformed the effect of the space, turning it from a 1990s loft shell into the semblance of a 1660s grand hall. The flat ceiling over the entrance was removed to reveal a high, pyramid-shaped ceiling, now painted royal blue with a pattern of gold fleur-de-lis. The ceiling of the living area was similarly removed, to expose

Warm ambient lighting is an important part of Caroline's design concept, as bright, modern fixtures and fittings would appear historically and aesthetically anachronistic.

attractive beams and four eaves. Rather than being disguised, the original stone fireplace was opened, restored and made a focal point of the scheme. Waiting their turn to be given Caroline's Baroque interpretation, the tall school windows will lend themselves to the flamboyant treatment she has in store for them.

Theatrical Furniture The scale of these features is also compatible with the monumental furniture that Caroline favours for its theatricality and grandeur: 'over-scaled items are always a favourite of mine, a trade secret learned from Douglas Adams.' The entrance hall doubles as an office by virtue of a massive eighteenth-century walnut cabinet housing a computer and other business paraphernalia, and a massive marble table in the kitchen (measuring 3 x 1.4m) conceals an oven and hob and can easily seat sixteen.

Guest Comforts Like many loft-dwellers, Caroline is fond of socializing with friends. In creating the mezzanine, her aim was to provide separate quarters where guests can relax with every comfort, including their own bathroom. The soaring ceiling with its honey-coloured wooden beams gives the mezzanine bedroom the appearance of a full-sized room, an effect heightened by Caroline's bold addition of a king-sized bed and a massive carved oak chest that makes an ornate and commodious bedside table.

Gentle flame-like lights show off the collection of fine art and furniture to best effect, the hall lantern here limning the walnut posts of the eighteenth-century cabinet that houses Caroline's office.

The gallery-style mezzanine, with its ornate wooden balustrades, offers cosy and inviting guest quarters that have all the intimacy and comfort of a double bedroom.

Disparate objects – a painted fairground banister (top), and classical *putto* (above) – seem perfectly matched within the exuberant historicism of this scheme.

Antiques and Effects   This decorative scheme could so easily have become pastiche, but Caroline has chosen to furnish her apartment with original seventeenth-century objects – Old Master paintings, oak cabinets, a four-poster bed, pewter tableware, architectural salvage and antiques – as well as items that would have been in evidence in a grand Baroque interior: blue and white china and tiles; needlepoint textiles; and orange trees. These she has blended with consummate flair to make her apartment look individual – and it is certainly quite different from those in the rest of the Tabard.

Paint Magic   Surprisingly, given the sumptuousness of the finished look, Caroline didn't spend a fortune on the fit-out. Some of the grandest effects have been produced with her own paintbrush, including the *trompe-l'oeil* 'stone' entrance hall and kitchen cupboards (standard kitchen units in heavy disguise.) Even the radiators are gold, a characteristically opulent and humorous touch. But Caroline hasn't finished yet – ultimately, the blue-painted ceiling will be frescoed with a sky scene. Currently, copies of ceiling and wall paintings from Vaux le Vicomte appear on the doors and overdoors to stunning and graceful effect.

Artful Illusion   All structural alterations have been heavily disguised so as to appear part of the fabric of the original building. So, for example, two storage cupboards built on either side of the hall and connected by six large overhead storage spaces make a visual doorway that divides the entrance/office area from the kitchen. These are finished with the same *trompe-l'oeil* rustication as the rest of the hall, thus cleverly suggesting that the apartment has massive, castle-thick walls throughout.

Unlike many mezzanines that look like insertions, Caroline's guest quarters appear rather to be a traditional upper storey with gallery, an effect aided by the grand, decorative fairground banister that Caroline bought from architectural salvage (and has preserved in its appealing distressed state). The carved oak strapwork panels that border the mezzanine floor also contribute to its appearance of structural permanence.

Caroline describes the look she has achieved as 'very masculine, heavy and colourful at the same time', but in fact the overall effect of the apartment is of beauty, warmth and comfort. Instead of seventeenth-century rushes, a new wool carpet was laid throughout the loft, except in the living room, where a large and luxurious antique Donegal rug conceals most of the wooden floor.

Tucked neatly behind the bedroom, Caroline's private en suite bathroom, though essentially modern, benefits from the same Baroque inspiration as the rest of the apartment – the final touch in a luxurious dream loft.

The Private Annexe In place of the original small single door in the corner of the living room, Caroline has made a substantial double door, which constitutes the principal feature of the wall – again decorated with oak strapwork panels bought from salvage. This leads to her elegant bedroom, bathroom and dressing room, three areas carefully designed to use the space of the original third room to maximum advantage. An oblique wall displays the silk hangings of the seventeenth-century four-poster bed to great effect, behind which are stored Caroline's fine clothes and large collection of shoes. The adjacent bathroom, though windowless, seems bright by virtue of the light-coloured and mirrored walls and Delft-style fresh blue and white tiles that were painted by a friend, William Pounds.

In this private annexe, filled with the soft textures, warm colours and exquisite objects, Caroline has created her own 'bower of bliss', a haven from modern stresses and discomforts. The effect here, though rigorously Baroque, is distinctly feminine: warm, sensuous and secluded. In this suite of rooms, Caroline has flouted the open-plan aesthetic of loft living by treating a domestic-scale space with palace-scale largesse.

A Perfectionist's Paradise Possibly Caroline will never finish her apartment, as she is loath to stop improving and refining her work. The curator of her own historic interior, she is always mindful both of the detail and of the overall effect. Each object, treatment and texture must find its place in the grand scheme of her imaginative playground.

de metzanine

**Strong geometry and industrial chic for a
hip city loft created on a tight budget**

I complete contrast with Caroline Haelterman's historic interior in the previous chapter, the journalist Matthew Jones's apartment – in the same converted Victorian school building in south London – is spare and modern. When looking to move out of his crowded flat in north London, Matthew knew that he wanted more space and was attracted by the idea of loft living, but was unsure of how to find a 'real' loft, i.e. a shell apartment in a fine, converted building. Guided by his friends, Julian de Metz and Amit Green of de Metz Green Architects, he viewed a number of properties, but was overwhelmed by the potential of one of the smaller units in the Tabard in Bermondsey (see page 84). It consisted of 72m² of two enormous, unmodified former classrooms and boasted fine views of Tower Bridge. Julian observes of the developer Sapcote's school conversions: 'These are probably as close to real lofts as you can get in London at the moment. They're central, but still represent reasonably good value for money.'

The stairs (below) have an enclosed banister of the same material and depth as the mezzanine balustrade, so that the mezzanine appears to extend down to the lower floor.

Financial Constraints   Julian and Amit were instantly engaged by the idea of turning these rooms into a single, coherent loft space, and Matthew more than happy to let them get to work on this enticing blank interior canvas: whitewashed walls and a wooden floor. However, having bought the shell, Matthew's budget was so limited that Julian and Amit were faced with a target expenditure of half the norm. But they remained positive, Amit observing, 'It's quite a challenge to work with limited resources, but it's also exciting to see what can be achieved.'

As budget options have always been the basis of 'real' loft living – the artists of New York would blanch at the idea of fitting out a loft for half a million – in practice, the budgetary constraint proved a creative spur for Julian and Amit. They decided to increase the space to around 90m² through the addition of a mezzanine platform, but to keep costs down by using budget materials and fittings: plyboard, render and paint; industrial free-standing kitchen units and the most basic sanitary ware in the bathroom.

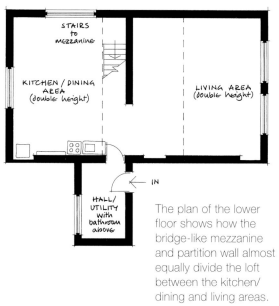

The plan of the lower floor shows how the bridge-like mezzanine and partition wall almost equally divide the loft between the kitchen/dining and living areas.

The Mezzanine Part of the original partition wall and the double door that divided the space into two rooms was removed to create a connected kitchen/dining and living area on the ground floor. Straddling this – positioned in the centre of the space so as to be clear of the massive 3m-high windows – is a mezzanine platform that commands fantastic views of the gritty urban landscape and of the City across the Thames.

Perhaps because the shallow mezzanine floor (only 100mm thick) is completely concealed and no beams are visible, the mezzanine appears monumental and solid, like a wooden beam across the width of the room or a free-standing sculptural element floating between two voids. Further heightening the sculptural effect are the large rectangular openings in the central wall that allow natural light to flood from one space to another.

The clean, architectonic lines of the mezzanine give it almost the quality of painting that – as in the canvas just visible to the right – uses geometric abstraction to make a strong visual impact.

Factory Features   The robust economical materials chosen have led the architects towards an industrial aesthetic: the surface-mounted service conduits and light fittings are of galvanized steel (cheaper than stainless); the internal partition wall is finished with rough-cast rendering (in pleasing contrast with the smooth birch ply); and the kitchen wall grit-blasted to its bare, original state.

While stripping back to basics and introducing inexpensive materials, the architects have also been careful to ensure a fine finish, for example in exposing the endgrain of the birch-faced ply, which creates an attractive sandwich appearance to the banister facings. The handrail that extends right around the mezzanine gallery is made of galvanized steel, to stunning effect.

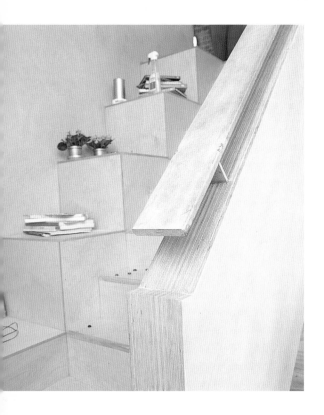

Open and Enclosed   By enclosing the mezzanine in this way, Julian and Amit have made the upper space semi-private. The open-plan bedroom/study area is not fully visible from the lower spaces, though air and light can circulate freely between floors. Amit describes the safe, 'cupped' feeling of the bedroom, with the bed neatly slotted between a deep render wall and the birch-ply surface of the mezzanine gallery.

The ingenious stepped storage boxes-cum-seats flanking the stairs provide useful resting places for objects in transit between floors, and have as pleasing an appearance as a neat arrangement of children's bricks.

A School Kitchen   By contrast, the cooking area is completely open to the lower living space. At first Julian and Amit were keen to install some sort of fitted units that could conceal the somewhat incongruous cast-iron fireplace on the kitchen wall, but finally decided instead on free-standing, stainless steel catering units – the kind found in school kitchens. The fireplace then was restored to use, as Matthew had originally wanted, and a further original feature – a Victorian ventilation grille – turned into an extractor fan. As Matthew is both an expert cook and an attentive host, a mobile stainless steel preparation table – like those dinner ladies serve from – was also bought to allow him to prepare food in the living area or wherever else he might want to chat to his guests. While satisfying the client's desire for professional-standard fittings, all the kitchen fixtures cost half the price of a fitted kitchen and better preserve the original character of the space. Even Matthew's enormous Bosch fridge – his one great extravagance – finds its niche within an original decorative arch. The main

The commercial catering units are exactly what one would expect to find in a school kitchen, but are equally in keeping with the pared-down, functional chic of the loft. The lighting conduit usefully serves as a hanging rack, and the recess beside the chimney-breast offered ready-made housing for a stylish Bosch fridge.

kitchen storage is provided by an open stainless steel shelf that runs the length of the kitchen area, but this space is supplemented by a commodious larder that sits cheek by jowl with Matthew's freezer in the apartment's neat, enclosed entrance hall. (Julian insisted that the hall be small and compact so that on entering the flat one emerges, dramatically, from a dark, intimate space into a light, cavernous one.)

Sensible Lighting Lighting was chosen on the basis of its having an industrial look and a reasonable price tag. The galvanized steel bulkhead lamps that range along the upper walls (and are also used as task lighting in the cooking area) cost less than an average bedside lamp, and the fluted glass pendant lamps that diffuse a warm light are a 1930s industrial classic – not dissimilar from classroom lighting of the sixties and seventies. Details such as these, while perfectly in keeping with the contemporary, industrial aesthetic, give the space a retro feel, as if the loft had been designed before the days of black leather and chrome modernism. Their initial brief from Matthew was: 'to create something contemporary and interesting without resorting to the obvious stereotypes of glass, bricks, white walls and shiny stainless steel fittings.' In fact, so careful have the architects been to avoid modernist clichés, that they have even used mill-finished garden uplighters to floodlight the upper spaces.

The Wooden Bathroom The bathroom is a further happy casualty of the limited budget. Rather than being tiled, it is clad in what *The Sunday Times* newspaper has described as de Metz Green's 'signature birch plywood', which is a cheaper and, in the context, a far more attractive solution. Originally, Matthew had wanted a separate bathroom and lavatory, but, when the architects devised a way of the bathroom being accessible

Clad in birch ply, the bathroom (left) has a restrained elegance. In place of decorative trimmings are practical features, such as the deck-mounted taps, swivel mixer spout and capacious Belfast sink (below).

The niche-like openings (right) in the mezzanine partition wall transmit light and air, serve as frames for display, and – with their simple geometric forms – have a strongly sculptural impact.

without guests having to walk through the bed area, he was happy to go with the simpler option of a single room. The bathroom fittings cost less than those in an average suburban home – without any compromise of comfort or practicality. The utilitarian Belfast sink is big enough to bath a child in, with taps and spout neatly mounted into a birch-ply deck.

Contrasts   The colours in the apartment are muted but warm. The rich and varied tones of the exposed bricks, the honey-coloured floorboards with their beeswax polish, the sand-coloured render and the pinkish birch ply all contribute to a mellow glow. The variety of textures also helps to highlight the particular beauties of each material. The architects observe that 'placing a smooth material next to a rougher one accentuates the innate quality of each', and the juxtaposition of the powdery render throughout the loft and the

The original fireplace is unmodified, the proportions, colours and textures of its plain surround and simple grate almost a template for the palette and materials chosen for the current interior. Only the iron roundel, with its quintessentially Victorian London Board Schools' insignia, seems of another era.

sculpturally smooth birch ply offers the most striking example of this principle of contrasts.

Raking sunlight flooding in the enormous bare windows further accentuates this textural play and creates ever-moving patterns around the sculptural mezzanine floor. As Julian says, 'the raw materials of design are scale and proportion' and he and Amit have made the brilliant natural light in the apartment a main criterion in determining how the space should be divided. The openings in the mezzanine walls both transmit light and frame interesting views, and the architects have ensured that, even in the bath, it is possible to spy Tower Bridge.

Detail and Design   The apartment may look spare and streamlined but is surprisingly rich in architectural detail, one example of the architects' inventiveness being the stepped ply storage boxes that border the stairway, doubling as seats. Another is the use of conduits in the kitchen area as a hanging rack for cooking utensils. As a result of such careful and well-thought-through design, this apartment has little need of furniture: a kitchen/dining table, a few chairs, a sofa and a bed are the only items necessary to make the space habitable and comfortable.

In designing this loft the architects were very much aware of the need to strike a balance between a respect for the original Victorian schoolroom space and the need to meet modern residential requirements. As Julian explains: 'The problem is how, rationally, to preserve the space, which has been bought and the buyer loves, and retain as much of its original character as possible, while giving it a residential character as well. The solution is good design.'

In this apartment good design hasn't been hindered by financial constraints. In fact, when Julian asks Amit what he would have done had more money been available, the answer is that a larger budget might well have ruined the project, detracting from the pure solutions exigency forced them to achieve. As he put it, with characteristic modesty, 'We just enjoyed being pragmatic and working with what was there.'

The eschewing of a residential look has meant that De Metz's design would be as fitting for an art gallery, office or airport as for a home. In the design of the stairway, less means more scope for freedom from interiors 'idioms'.

milano
magnifico

A former factory in Italy's industrial north, opened to reveal a traveller's rich treasury of antiques and collectables

This Milanese loft is highly unorthodox. Comprising the entire upper storey of a former factory, the floor plan offers the open and communicative areas that have become fashionable in Italian conversions, but the décor gives the apartment the busy intimacy of an old family home.

In creating this interior, the designer Thierry Oliver specifically set out to make it special, a reflection of the adventurous spirit of its owner, a long-time friend with whom Thierry has spent many happy voyages overseas. Indeed, travel is the leitmotiv that unifies the many and various exotic objects that furnish the apartment, making a home in which a larger-than-life figure, such as Ernest Hemingway, might feel at ease.

Moderno/Classico   The whole apartment is imbued with a sense of largesse: warm and welcoming, luxurious and sumptuous, old and modern. Thierry is no purist. His aesthetic is governed not by decorative correctness, but by a sense of how the space can best meet the practical and spiritual needs of its occupant. Thus the ultra-modern mezzanine – rising like a great sculptural centrepiece in the principal living area – supports a study traditionally furnished with built-in bookshelves, a Victorian desk, chair and chaise-longue and a fine kelim that warms the effect of the highly polished parquet flooring. Here old and new merge unashamedly, and the mezzanine – its classically modern looks resembling the deck of a liner – offers an unusual and pleasantly open space for what is

Unlike many lofts, this apartment has a number of quite conventionally configured rooms, but is dominated (as the plan below shows) by the large main living area. The striking spiral stairs lead to the mezzanine styled like a traditional study (below right) – an unusual digression from modernist loft aesthetics.

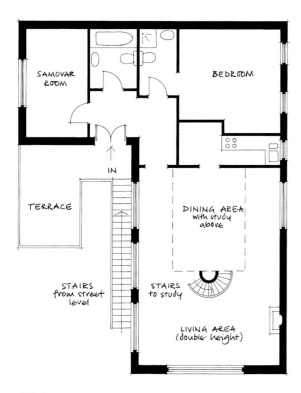

The juxtaposition of a prominent modern mezzanine and antique furnishings isn't visually jarring, partly because the nautical look of the banister and railings lends the whole the atmosphere of a 1920s luxury liner.

essentially a conventional design treatment. The novelty lies not in the treatment itself, but in Thierry's confident and conscious courting of contrast.

The industrial shape and scale of the main living space again offers scope for surprise. The barrel-vault ceiling is a legacy of the building's industrial use, yet lends an elegance to an interior rich in antiques and fine textiles. A further juxtaposition is offered by the mezzanine supports, which Thierry uses to create a 'virtual' dining room directly under the mezzanine. Though open and communicative with the rest of the living room, the dining area feels private and intimate, conducive to long meals and fine conversation.

An eclectic collection eclectically lit: a variety of wooden *oggetti* cluster in the glow of a Japanese vase lamp (above) and a focused beam illuminates a delicate glass sculpture in a pillar recess in the dining area (top).

Minor Modification The windows are the only modern, industrial feature to have been modified for the sake of continuity with the residential look of the interior. Factory-style but made of attractive Douglas pine, they flood the space with light at all times of the day, so Thierry can afford to veil them with white cotton sheers that temper what might otherwise be the heavy look of the grid-like frames. Blending well with the almond yellow plaster walls, these sheers have an airiness and mobility against which the solid antique furniture and copious ornaments make a graceful contrast.

The antiques and objects collected over a lifetime of travel and adventure give this former factory the relaxed, colonial look of a gentlemen's club.

Visual Mix   Thierry's lighting of this space is also eclectic, to say the least, the recessed downlighters under the mezzanine being supplemented by gilt and glass wall lights, a pendent shade in the niche created by the mezzanine staircase, and a traditional chandelier – all within a few paces of each other. Although unusual, this mixture of styles – evident even in the lighting – defines the peculiar charm of this apartment. Thierry wanted 'to create the atmosphere of an English traveller', hence disparate objects find themselves housemates by virtue of their collectability. With their inviting warm pink hue, the Regency-style leather armchairs (which were actually made in the 1930s) are a focal point around which possessions from the owner's former houses happily congregate: for example, an elliptical rosewood table; an oriental sculpture of an elephant; and a lamp made from a nineteenth-century Japanese vase. Objects from various epochs contribute to a look that reflects the owner's varied taste and Thierry has been careful not to stifle the individual 'voices' of these pieces. He observes, 'For my part I have tried to give the objects a life of their own within the context.'

Oriental Digressions   Nowhere is this reverence to the owner's collection more evident than in the principal bedroom, which is oriental by virtue of its furnishings rather than any architectural detailing. Certainly the Moroccan frieze above the bed and the narrow rectangular windows are in keeping with the ethnic treatment chosen, but they are of secondary importance to the furnishings. Like the living area, this room does not have an archetypal 'loft look'. The high ceiling – again barrel vaulted – just makes for a spacious feel.

The international feel of this loft is created in large part by distinctive and exotic objects and materials: oriental textiles (left); a Moroccan overdoor (below); an Empire-style chaise-longue (below left); and a Turkish samovar (far left).

The suntrap terrace, with its high, exposed deck and casual deckchairs, is a complete change in style from the treasure-filled interior. Increasingly, roof gardens are being seen as essential to comfortable and convivial loft dwelling.

Here the interest focuses on the bed – modern, but with an oriental-style bedhead and bolster covered in an opulent antique flat-weave textile that is used again to upholster the nineteenth-century footstools that flank the bed. Most unusual of all is a Moroccan portal in painted wood that makes a shrine-like side table. The effect of these rich textures and patterns is to make this bedroom seem secluded and intimate, the antithesis of the open bed platforms found in many modern loft conversions.

Tailor-made Spaces   Just as the decoration and furnishing of this loft is unusual and highly individual, so the layout reflects the particular desires of the owner, meeting his need for a large, open-plan reception space, but also for enclosed, private areas, for example the modestly sized Samovar Room, which, with its Turkish silver samovar, is dedicated to the pursuit of gentle pleasures: tea drinking, reading and conversation.

Again by way of contrast, the visitor to this Milanese treasure house emerges from the sumptuous and enveloping interior into the dazzling light of the suntrap roof terrace, where shocking pink deckchairs provide an unexpectedly modern and informal touch. Many lofts have the benefit of roof terraces but few have such a country atmosphere. With comfort again as the key, this outdoor room (complete with roof that echoes the barrel vaulting indoors) is essentially a green space, a container garden inviting complete relaxation.

Externally, this loft has an unusual casket shape, an apt visual metaphor because it is indeed like a sturdy treasure chest – relatively plain on the outside, but containing rich and varied spoils in dizzying profusion.

Past printworks, present
loft: an unconventional
family home that bends
1930s' style to a twenty-
first-century lifestyle

space
invaders

n the heart of London's Clerkenwell, an area traditionally dedicated to light industry, stands a good-looking 1930s industrial building that was originally a printworks. An obvious advantage of such a building over a traditional warehouse (used for storage) is its enormous windows, designed to provide maximum natural light to the work floor, and the resulting double-height ceilings.

The building was in such a poor state of repair that it had been scheduled for demolition, but its concrete frame structure, huge metal-framed windows, and its location in Clerkenwell – fast becoming the focus of SoHo-style loft spaces in London – made it an attractive site for conversion into residential loft apartments.

Form Meets Function   In 1993 Manhattan Lofts, the company Harry Handelsman founded with the aim of expanding loft living in Britain, undertook to develop this modern gem into over twenty shell units. As the developer, Manhattan was sensitive to the original industrial aesthetic: the exterior was rendered and painted white; the entrance doors are simple, large and metal-framed; the communal spaces minimally decorated and the lift of functional, gleaming steel. The look is wholeheartedly unfussy and metropolitan, prey to none of the design solecisms that can so easily be committed in the name of comfort and luxury.

The plans of the lower (below) and upper (below right) floors of this double-decker apartment show the interesting mix of open-plan living areas and private enclosed rooms. From the mezzanine one can look down on to the kitchen and the enormous 'front of house' living space.

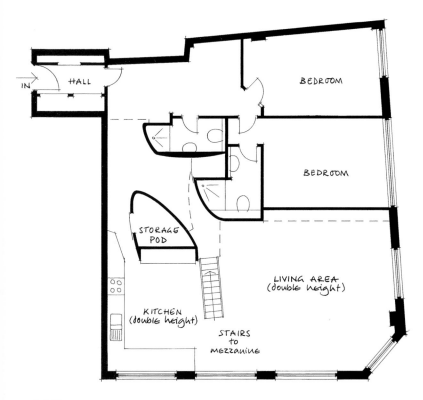

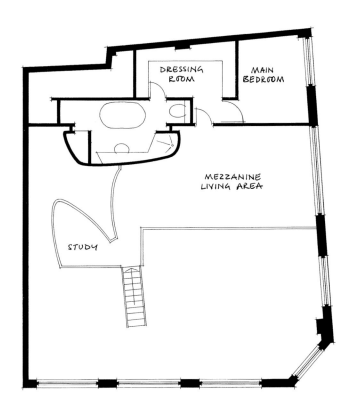

Designed as a printworks, with appropriately large windows to allow maximum light on to the work floor, this 1930s building (below) has an industrial beauty perfectly in keeping with the ideals of stylish, design-based loft apartments.

A fish-eye lens has captured the truly extraordinary openness of the stadium-like living space (above), in which furnishings are kept to a minimum and the impressive full-height windows left entirely untreated.

Retail Tenants   Appropriately, the ground floor is inhabited by businesses that complement this environment. Circus, the architectural practice well known for its loft interiors (having completed over fifty fit-outs in London), shares the floor with Viaduct, the contemporary furniture retailer, which has an enormous showroom stretching around the corner of the building, and a graphic design studio. The spare and elegant interiors of these commercial spaces serve as an exciting taster of what can be achieved within the soaring residential spaces above.

Loft Livers   Although sited in an area that is increasingly thought of as London's artistic centre, the Summer's Street development is not inhabited by those whom admen so often choose to depict in loft spaces – musicians, artists and other hip urbanites – but by people from all walks of life and of all ages who have turned architectural shells into comfortable, if unconventional, homes.

A low-ceilinged, utilitarian landing betrays nothing of the splendour that lies behind the door of the double shell bought by Su and Paul Vaight in 1993 and converted by the architects, Circus, into a single 225m² apartment. Playing on discrepancies of scale, Circus designed a small, windowless hall as the entrance to the apartment, which, painted black and lit only by jewel-like halogen bulbs, opens into the bright, soaring space of the loft.

Modern classics, such as the Le Corbusier dining table (right) are only one element in a scheme that bucks all orthodoxies. What Le Corbusier would have made of the meander pattern in the soft carpet and Dawn Dupree's bright textile banners (far right) is hard to imagine, but the Vaights blend the purist and pure fun with appropriately gay abandon.

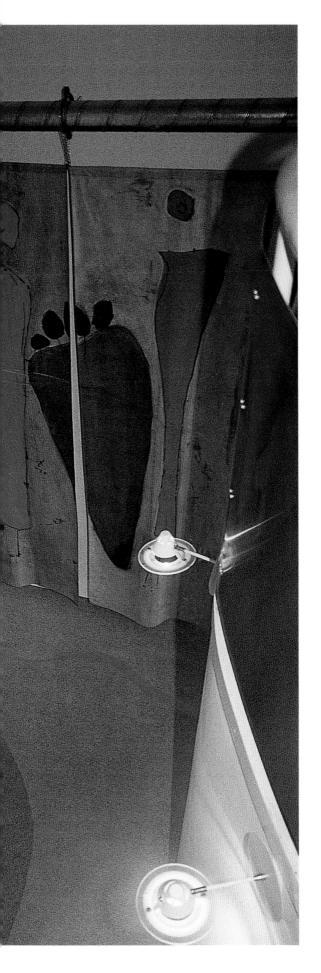

Reaching the Space Age   Su and Paul are very far from being stereotypical loft dwellers. Having lived in rented accommodation abroad and then in a three-storey Victorian semi in Kent, they decided to jettison the detritus of suburban family life. Selling almost all of their furniture and ridding themselves of the clutter of decades, they made a fresh start and a wholehearted commitment to urban living. Yet this elegant and orderly apartment lacks none of the comforts of a family home. The loft has three bedrooms, each with its own bathroom – a must for the two then teenage children – and an informal sitting area on the mezzanine that invites sprawling relaxation.

Emanating Warmth   The Vaights worked closely with Circus to achieve a look that is at once spare and industrial and warm and inviting. Wooden floors work well in lofts, being in keeping with a utilitarian aesthetic but more comfortable than most other hard floor surfaces, and, accordingly, the principal living area of this apartment has a mellow maple floor. Adjoining this, however, is an area of sensuous carpeting by Helen Yardley, which, with its meandering abstract pattern and gentle colours, marks a transition between the hall and living areas, and softens and warms the overall look of the lower floor. The gas-fired heating system under the maple raises it slightly higher than the carpet, so that one steps down into a soft pool of warmth and colour that flows through to the more intimate bedroom spaces at the rear of the apartment.

Whitewashing such a large space would have made it too stark and inhospitable, so light but warm colours were chosen for the walls and the ceiling: trusty magnolia to the level of the mezzanine railing and warm apricot above. Circus recommended that the Vaights avoid hanging many pictures so as not to interrupt the huge, calm expanses of wall space, and the resulting look is uncluttered and roomy, with the walls serving to open out rather

The utility pod (above) makes a witty and up-front statement about the aesthetic exuberance but also the basic practicality of this apartment. Resembling a space-ship or an industrial installation, it is in fact a wonderfully useful 'glory hole', filled with mops, brooms and supplies of dog food.

than to close in the apartment. The only wall decoration Su and Paul introduced is a triptych of full-height, exquisitely coloured textile designs by Dawn Dupree that hang like banners beside the kitchen.

Unusual Utility   Circus has carefully avoided one of the common pitfalls in a loft of this size – the tendency for furnishings to appear diminished and insignificant – by subtly interrupting the cavern-like space. The transition from enclosed hall to wide open living area is made less stark by what is possibly the most unusual element of the apartment: a smooth and curvaceous utility 'pod'. This houses and hides all the usual domestic clutter and peering into this useful little space is oddly reassuring – amid the stunning glamour of the Vaights' loft there is still a place for the impedimenta of everyday living. And this pod is doubly functional, being surmounted by a neat, gently curving workstation level with the mezzanine.

Another witty feature that plays on a high-tech aesthetic is the projecting stairway. Its skeletal iron structure and the oblique angle of its projection into the room makes it feel light and temporary, almost as if these were the boarding stairs of an aeroplane.

Seen from the mezzanine, the kitchen appears neat and functional, with a fresh yet gentle colour scheme that makes it easy on the eye, as part of the open-plan living area.

Nautical References

Like the pod, which somewhat resembles a funnel, the other most important architectural element – the metal-spined staircase, designed with the help of structural engineers Battle McCarthy – has a nautical feel, and appears rather like the gangway of a ship. Its slightly oblique position avoids a crude partitioning of the loft into room-like segments, but nevertheless serves to divide the kitchen area from the main living space. And the metal ribs of this staircase are cleverly echoed and played upon by the skeletal lighting rig, specially designed by Circus and Box Products, that defines a visual 'ceiling' for the kitchen.

The Retro Kitchen

The kitchen treatment is often the greatest challenge presented by a loft. A modern fitted kitchen can look out of place in the context of an industrial space, so the Vaights and Circus strove for a solution that would be both functional and appropriate. By chance they came across a 1950s kitchen that was being stripped from an unmodernized flat in Hyde Park, the metal doors and drawers being in a distinctive early modern style and of reasonable condition. These were restored and neatly fitted along one wall, surmounted by a worktop and splashback of pre-moulded

Corian, above which runs a strip of glass sand-blasted to a greenish hue. The slightly retro style of the units is complemented by the huge, bright blue Boffi fridge, resplendent in its own housing (an echo of the sculptural solidity of the utility pod).

Modern Classics   The formality of the main living area is achieved not by opulence but by restraint. A very few pieces of brightly coloured fine modern furniture define

the space. A Matthew Hilton chair and coffee table, Philippe Starck stacking chairs, a curvilinear deep blue Dutch sofa (which echoes the colour of the fridge) and a Le Corbusier dining table create a breathtaking gallery of furniture art. The height of modern elegance, this lower space reflects a combination of moods that might be said to define the best of loft living.

The Public/Private Mezzanine   The major architectural insertion was the mezzanine, which houses an informal family living area, the small workstation (above the pod), and the Vaights' bedroom and bathroom. In this apartment differences of scale are used to dramatic effect, and on the mezzanine the spaces are more confined and the mood intimate. The modestly sized bedroom is completely enclosed, and

The Vaights have tended to choose furniture – such as the blue Dutch sofa (above) – which, although it is unmistakably contemporary, is nevertheless in keeping with the Art Deco style and proportions of the building.

is decorated with oriental rugs and furniture in a style quite distinct from the rest of the apartment. Almost of the same size is the adjacent dressing room, comfortingly stuffed with a disorderly assortment of clothes. These are definitely private quarters, cosy and relaxing, and with an internal bathroom, where, at the flick of a light switch, radio is broadcast through built-in car stereo speakers.

The Youth Zone   Beneath this area, on the lower level of the apartment and in a zone of their own, are the children's bedrooms, which reflect their inhabitants' very different tastes. This is very much an apartment that invites invention and individuality: daughter Harriet's bathroom, for example, has a jazzy floor of multi-coloured rubber tiles and walls that look as if there has been an explosion in a sweet factory. Even the loo seat is kitsch and quirky, with its frilly sunflower effect and joky Perspex lid.

A Life-enhancing Look   Su Vaight describes the look she aimed to create as 'bright, energizing and happy', and she has achieved it through the exploitation of natural light, the creation of a free-flowing but varied living space, the use of bright and invigorating colours, and a focus on clean, pleasing forms.

Like a modern-day priest hole, the Vaights' bathroom (above) is completely enclosed. With every comfort (even wall-mounted car speakers), this private zone offers the luxury that today's loft-dwellers expect.

Daughter Harriet's bathroom (right) is a fine demonstration of how colourful and fanciful it is possible to be in modern lofts.

reservoir
docks

**Living with 200 years of
history: the conversion
of the most important
warehousing in
London's Docklands**

Built in 1802 by Napoleonic prisoners of war, the West India Docks were London's first dockside warehouses, used to receive valuable cargoes of oil, spirits, sugar, molasses, tea and coffee, imported from the West Indies. The original warehouse system consisted of a series of enormous buildings. A number of these were destroyed during wartime bombing, but what remains is nevertheless vast, extending from West India Dock around the curve of the Thames westward to the Limehouse Link.

The façade of the Port East apartments (right) is intentionally austere and prison-like because the warehouses were intended to house and protect precious cargoes from theft.

The new footbridge (below) that links Port East to Canary Wharf is an award-winning example of design bravado. In blatant contrast to the sombre, weathered brick, it is a symbol of the vigorous new use to which the buildings are being put.

Historic Significance   Being the only surviving and untouched multi-storey brick warehousing from this period, the Port East Apartments are Grade I listed. So important is their regeneration that the project has the endorsement of the Department of the Environment, the Royal Fine Art Commission and English Heritage – bodies dedicated to the preservation of its unique original features, which include the distinctive spike-framed windows that protected the goods from theft. The consortium of developers that have taken on the site – Manhattan Loft Corporation, Marylebone Warwick Balfour and London and Easter Properties – are therefore faced with the exciting challenge of preserving an historic monument while creating a new urban village that will serve residential, commercial, recreational and retail interests.

Regeneration When complete, it is envisaged that the redevelopment will provide over 106 loft apartments, 6500m² of restaurants, bars and shops and, appropriately, the new Museum of the Docklands, which is scheduled to open in 2000. New buildings to the north will house a supermarket and a ten-screen cinema, and West India Tower – thirty-two storeys of curved glass – will be built to the east in exciting contrast to the late Georgian architecture of the warehouses. The scheme is intended to regenerate the entire quayside, with improved amenities and recreational facilities creating jobs and a cultural focus for the area.

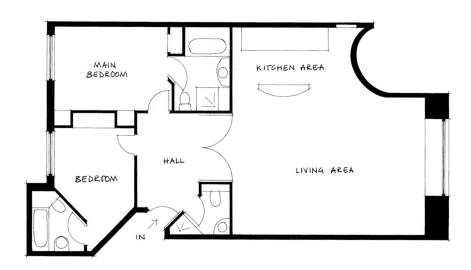

In the original plans for the development of Canary Wharf, immediately to the east, the space in front of the warehouses was earmarked for a large entertainments development, but luckily this did not go ahead and the warehouses will retain their correct relationship with the quayside. Restaurants and cafés will now be able to offer *al fresco* dining, and it is intended that this space should become a lively pedestrian plaza, a hub of social activity, and the site of cultural festivals. This area is connected to the now bustling Canary Wharf by Future Systems' high-tech bridge that glows frog green at night.

The plan (above) of this single-storey, single-height apartment shows how the space is half open and half divided into discrete rooms – a neat arrangement that simultaneously offers the conviviality of a loft and the privacy of a flat. The bedroom windows look out on to the building's new central atrium.

The building's Grade I listing means that all its important architectural features, such as the timber beams and iron stanchions (right), may not be altered in any way. Happily, it is just such features that make for attractive loft conversions in historic buildings like these.

Fitted-out Apartments So large a development is Port East – five huge, connected blocks – that it is being realized in stages. The apartment featured here is in block B, which, with A and C, is being developed first. These three blocks are similar in type, having oak beams, pitch-pine

Height is the most notable feature of most lofts, but in the Port East apartments it is the depth of space that is most striking. In keeping with the exposed wood and brick of the expansive living area, Joanna Skoczynska has chosen almost exclusively to use natural materials for the furnishings, such as cotton, leather and antique wood.

joists and, other than the penthouses, single-height ceilings. Again, because of the historic importance of the building, the apartments are not being sold as shells, but fully fitted out to a very high general specification. This apartment is therefore representative of the architect's (Alison Clark of AJC Designs) vision of the look of the interior of the apartments as a whole, with limestone and wood floors, exposed brick walls and high-tech modern fittings, finishes and appliances.

A distinct buyer profile is emerging, the majority of purchasers being professional men of between about thirty and forty-five, many of whom work in Canary Wharf or in the City. The look is well suited to this market: functional and unfussy, in keeping with the warehouse aesthetic, but also relaxing and luxurious with a sophisticated, classically modern interior.

Creating Light   As the show flat, this two-bedroom, south-facing apartment is the template for the look. Alison Clark modestly observes that you can't go wrong with such a building as a basis, but in fact the smallish windows and deep floorplates (the unobstructed distance between the windows on either side of the building), combined with the planning restrictions, meant that the architect was

Against ancient oak beams a new, wooden fitted kitchen could look jarringly nouveau. This gleaming stainless steel kitchen, however, is appropriately industrial and visually strong enough to take its place beside the rough bricks and heavy beams. The sheen of the steel also helps maximize the light in a relatively dark part of the loft.

faced with the problem of there being limited natural light. The solution was to build an atrium in the centre of the building to provide light to the back of the apartments that may be enhanced by artificial daylight in dull conditions.

Sensitive Conversion That the original structure is far from square has meant that each apartment is different. The bathrooms have had to be designed along the joist runs, and English Heritage has stipulated that all partitions be 'demountable', so that it would be possible to return the building to its Georgian state.

As original, natural materials – in the red bricks, timber beams and iron stanchions – are the principal features of the space, Alison and the designer, Joanna Skoczynska, have tried to introduce only other natural materials into the interior, choosing in particular those that have a hand-made quality. The low bench in the living area, for example, was designed by Skoczynska and crafted from zinc and wood by the joiner Charlie Batho; the sofa is covered in natural linen; the chair in leather; and the rug hand-woven in Nepal and dyed with vegetable colours.

A predominance of wood makes for a warm, womb-like mood. Batho's oak shutters seem almost to be an extension of the fabric of the building. Oak is used with stainless steel in the shelves; the dining table has an extraordinary Escher-like wooden structure as its base; and an antique African bench makes a low table that reiterates the rough-hewn look of the exposed beams. Skoczynska observes that 'in furnishing this apartment the emphasis has been on the natural and the hand-made, but used in such as way as to create a chic environment that will appeal to urban, professional people.'

In keeping the mellow tones of the wood and the warm red of the bricks, the partition walls in the living area, hall and cloakroom have a subtle matt texture and a neutral tone, being coated with an unusual polished plaster made out of ground marble, pigments and wax.

A Social Space   The living and kitchen areas are open-plan to allow maximum circulation for the social interaction that is so important to the ethos of loft dwelling, and the original and very attractive curving brick wall forms a natural bay into which the kitchen very conveniently fits. Here again, Skoczynska has gone for a classically modern look. The predominance of stainless steel reflects and maximizes the light in this area, but is prevented

In the main bedroom (right) and the spare bedroom/study (below), designer Joanna Skoczynska has chosen light, smooth furnishings as a foil to the dark and richly textured wood and brick.

from appearing clinical by the informality of the the light-coloured timber of the units and the natural texture of the limestone floor. Low-level steel and glass pendent lamps also help to create a sense of intimacy in the area of the unusual cantilevered glass breakfast bar. Skoczynska and the kitchen supplier Neil Lerner have carefully avoided this bar having the appearance of a heavy object that divides the space. Its brushed steel sides reflect the warm natural tones of its surroundings, and the sparkling glass top looks almost weightless, like a great diaphanous wing. The challenge was to create a galley kitchen that was open and conducive to the theatre of cooking while accommodating the full complement of modern appliances, from a canopy extractor to an oven with a built-in microwave.

Marine associations, always appropriate in bathroom furnishings, are particularly suited to a wharfside warehouse. In the main bathroom (left) the porthole mirror and steel basin are subtly allusive. Here, as in the en suite bathroom (below), old materials meet new in an effective blend of cool modernity and rich history.

Custom Design   Across the spacious hall are two bedrooms of conventional size, each with an en suite bathroom. These have real windows that look into the inner atrium of the building. Again the bias of the furnishings is towards the natural and the hand made. In the master bedroom the bed was designed around the white mohair blanket that Joanna found in Liberty's, and was crafted from oak by Charlie Batho. Even the feather mattress was custom-made. Out of maple Charlie also constructed the chic bed/desk unit in the second bedroom, which was specifically designed for the space by Alison Clark. Light plaster walls make both rooms seem larger than they are, contrasting pleasingly with the rough, rich textures of the brick and beams.

The bathrooms are spare, chic and luxurious. Alison Clark designed the architectonic basin stands, Joanna Skoczynska all the other elements. It is in the principal bathroom that the contrast between old and new is most striking: the massive, grainy and rough-hewn beams preside over a smooth, cool, classically post-modern interior of glistening glass and steel.

Creating the Unexpected   This pilot Port East apartment has a very powerful atmosphere. Through the use of natural materials and textures, and, conversely, the unashamed modernism of the fixtures and fittings, the architect and designer have managed to highlight the fact that this loft sits within a unique historic building. Skoczynska delights in what she describes as 'the sense of the unexpected' whereby a friendly and comfortable home finds its place between bare brick walls and iron stanchions.

Calm simplicity – an architect's dream brief for a spacious loft in an industrial landscape

architectural
correctness

York Way is distinctly unresidential. Known by London cab drivers as the quickest route from north London into the heart of King's Cross, it is flanked by a strange patchwork of industrial units, yards, office buildings and the occasional pub. A few Victorian terraced houses, with barely a pelmet of grass to the pavement, come nowhere near making this a 'neighbourhood watch' area. And the views are as industrialized as any in the north of England, with the huge, landmark gas cylinders (now listed) rising up before the grimy, busy thoroughfare of King's Cross Station.

One wouldn't imagine this road to be a Mecca for the great and the glamorous, but one building here, York Central, is home to a number of very illustrious people. These include a world-renowned inventor and one of Britain's most famous photographers, who live here partly because of the raw urban beauty of the location.

The pragmatic International Modern style of this 1930s warehouse (right) has profoundly influenced Brookes Stacey Randall in the treatment of the living space (below). The architects, with Freddy Daniels, have chosen as far as possible to furnish it – or rather not to furnish it – in keeping with the monumentality and restraint of the building's exterior.

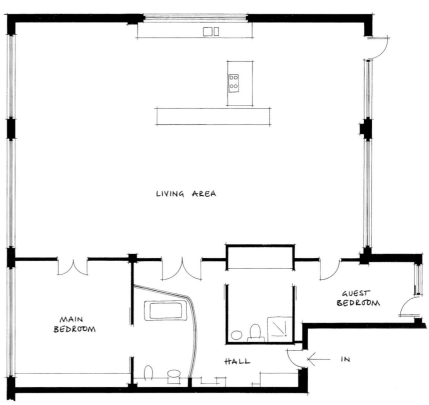

LIVING AREA

MAIN
BEDROOM

GUEST
BEDROOM

HALL

IN

When Freddy Daniels, a stockbroker, first visited York Central, he was refreshed by the unusual environment. Having come from a Georgian terrace in Islington and with most of his colleagues based in Kensington and Chelsea, King's Cross was a completely new prospect. So too was living in a warehouse space.

Former Uses   Built in the 1930s, York Central is a fine example of International Modern architecture at its most pragmatic. Built as an all-purpose warehouse – it was once used to store Remembrance Day poppies – the building's exterior is mimetic of its structure: a concrete frame supporting vast single-height spaces lit by wall-size windows.

Stately Modernity   In refurbishing the exterior of the block, London Buildings hasn't made any concessions to its residential use. The windows are now double-glazed but pivot open just like the originals. As might be expected, the residents have eschewed flouncy window treatments, so that, from the outside, York Central looks just as industrial, if somewhat more stately, than the other buildings on York Way.

Hidden from the road, but visible from the back of York Central, is King's Cross Marina around which several fine warehouse conversions, also by London Buildings, are part

As the floor plan (above) shows, one enters the loft between the red-walled guest bathroom and the glazed wall of Freddy Daniels' bathroom (see page 136) to be confronted by the vast living area that occupies more than half the loft's total floor space.

of a vast regeneration scheme. This waterside haven will introduce pubs, a theatre and restaurants to the area, and so – suddenly – the building will find itself close to London's newest colony of loft apartments.

The communal areas of York Central are Spartan but elegant, with a gleaming stainless steel lift, industrial-style light fittings and, again, not so much as a nod towards homeliness. If pure loft living today is about embracing the industrial aesthetic, then this is the seminary of London loft apartments.

Empty Space   When Freddy Daniels called in the architects Brookes Stacey Randall, this space was a 270m² shell: simply a vast empty rectangle with

Walls of window are left entirely bare, allowing the light to create ever-changing patterns over the smooth blond planes of wall and floor in the living area and adjacent bedroom (left).

concrete supporting pillars and large metal-framed windows. There was therefore complete freedom (within the usual building restraints) to create an interior exactly suited to Freddy's needs.

A Radical Footprint   As space and light were the most striking features of the unit, it was decided that the floor plan should be as open as possible. In practice, this meant combining the living, dining and kitchen areas into one huge space spanning the entire width of the building and occupying more than half the available floor area. As a single person, Freddy only needed one large bedroom and a study convertible to a bedroom for occasional guests. However, it was important to him that these rooms have separate bathrooms, to allow visitors comfort and privacy.

Boldly sited in the centre of the apartment, the broad, low-level kitchen (above) reiterates the wide, horizontal thrust of the space, and is designed to allow cooking to be the focus of Freddy Daniel's entertaining.

Too often architects are asked to carve loft spaces into three- and four-bedroom family homes. But here Paul Voysey, the project architect, Nik Randall, the partner in charge, and the rest of the design team were presented with a dream brief: a loft spacious and minimal but not cold and precious, in which a single person can relax, entertain and have fun.

Past Lives   Unusually, the starting point was Freddy's old flat, which, like most flats, contained a variety of objects in a range of styles. Nik Randall and his colleagues visited it and discussed it with Freddy, asking what he thought worked and didn't work and trying to pick up clues as to his tastes and needs – as Nik puts it, 'to understand how he lived and how he wanted to live'. This discussion proved profoundly helpful, giving Paul Voysey a starting point for some preliminary sketches.

On the basis of these, fundamental decisions were made. Brookes Stacey Randall originally suggested a galley-style kitchen in one corner, but Freddy (a keen cook) was adamant that the kitchen should be central to the living space, a social hub between the dining and living areas. Similarly, when the architects alighted on the idea of the guest bathroom being made to look like a red box from without – 'a subtle orientation device ' – Freddy loved the idea and insisted on keeping it in the plan. With over a year before the building work was due to begin, there was much time for the architect and client to collaborate over crucial details. Together they decided to situate the principal bedroom to the east to get the first dawn light, and the dining area to the west to catch the last rays of the setting sun.

Freddy's unusual post-modern en suite bathroom (left) is enclosed by illuminated etched glass, allowing light from his bedroom (below) to penetrate this minimalist sanctuary.

From the other side, the bathroom's softly lit wall of curved glass brings an unusual luminosity to the entrance hall, a prelude to the immense, light-filled living space beyond.

Flexible Zones The final floor plan was pleasingly simple: the bedrooms and bathrooms were to be accommodated between the entrance and the first set of columns, and this would leave the remaining vast kitchen/dining/living room, as desired, entirely open.

The idea was then to break down the notion of corridors and rooms within this fire-protected private area by making the spaces as interconnected and flexible as possible. A consistent feature of Brookes Stacey Randall's designs – consummately realized in Nik's own home (see Cool School, pages 73–81) – is to meet current desires but also to allow for future needs. Today Freddy can use the second room as an office, tomorrow it can be a guest bedroom, but it could equally well become a child's room in the future, and the design allows for further bedrooms to be accommodated into the main living space as and when necessary. As Nik neatly expresses it, they 'planned for the future, then retracted to what is needed now.'

Concepts A further similarity between this apartment and Nik's converted schoolhouse lies in the incorporation of colour, texture and opacity, which is used not just to please the eye, but architecturally to distinguish the various areas and their functions. The architects vividly describe how these qualities define the circulation in the space:

'The entrance is compressed. It passes from the front door between a grey-green storage wall and the terracotta box of the guest shower room. As one moves through it, the area lightens and widens, and the ceiling steps up. Daylight is diffused through the curved etched toughened glass wall of the bathroom. Wide double doors provide access to the main space, the whole scale of which is accentuated in contrast with the constricted approach.'

In one corner of the terrace a large, well-stocked container garden offers the pleasures of *al fresco* dining and summer leisure in the heart of an area of London better known for its gasworks than its green spaces.

Such conceptual thinking is the domain of the modern architect and it is unlikely that Freddy would have been able to frame such ideas alone. The beauty of this collaboration is in Brookes Stacey Randall tapping into the seam of his tastes, recognizing his exuberance, open-mindedness and independence and reflecting these qualities in his surroundings. The resulting apartment is distinctly chic but far from ostentatious. As the architects observe, 'it is only a statement about Freddy's enjoyment of life – not a pad intended to impress other people.' In Nik's view, creating a loft for a specific client is usually much more engaging than working to a developer's brief: 'the personal, emotional response is so important and rewarding for the architect – and both parties learn a lot in the process.'

Together, the client and architect have chosen to make the most of the building's original materials, exposing, sand-blasting and sealing the existing brick, and allowing the concrete ceiling and columns to remain pure white. The introduction of a western red cedar floor is unobtrusive, its rich hues blending well with the reddish tones of the brickwork, and the stainless steel kitchen surfaces look almost like industrial workbenches. Even the 180m² terrace, though with an elegant container garden in one corner, has basic concrete tiles little different from the originals.

No Baggage The move required Freddy to shed most of his belongings, and this he did willingly, also being prepared to live for a month with only a bed and a deckchair: 'fun for a while – the ultimate loft experience – but I was glad to sit down when the furniture finally arrived.' Even now, with Le Corbusier's famous tubular steel and leather Grand Confort chairs and sofa in place, the furnishings are minimal. The apartment is intended to be sparse and uncluttered (with the storage walls in the hall and bedroom providing more than ample space for the effects of a single man), so that the original warehouse look remains intact. Freddy's bicycle is perfectly at home here, and will soon be joined by his motorbike (which, admittedly, he rarely rides).

In some ways this is a hybrid loft: architect-designed but with the rawness and visual bite of the original shell left intact; comfortable and convenient but not homely in any conventional way. Here Freddy has the best of all possible worlds: space, light, and a profound sense of freedom from the mess and muddle of everyday life. When asked what impact the loft has had on his life, he remarks, with the utmost seriousness, 'I don't get such bad hangovers here.' One can quite imagine this to be true – the loft has a calm simplicity, tranquil without being dull and fun without being contrived. One can party with friends in the great social plane of the living area or relax in the quiet calm of the sanctuary-like bathroom.

Freddy has chosen to keep this expanse of terrace free of any kind of distraction from the gritty industrial view (right).

high drama

Purple passages and in-your-face kitsch: Glasgow's introduction to loft living

With its international reputation as a centre of design excellence, one would imagine that Glasgow would be replete with loft apartments. But this is far from the case. Until 1997, when the charismatic developer, Andrew Wadsworth of MetroLoft (part of The Waterhouse Group; see also The Top Storey, pages 52–9), turned his attention to the City of Architecture and Design 1999, not a single building had been converted into lofts. Back in 1984, Andrew was responsible for New Concordia Wharf, the first major development of lofts on the Thames, and, having undertaken many London loft conversions since then, was keen to import his knowledge to the Scottish urban scene.

The new Todd Building (below), though stylistically distinct from the old, reiterates the tall runs of windows and wide expanses of floor that are such a distinctive feature of the shells in the original block (bottom).

The Todd Building   The building that attracted his attention is typically Glaswegian – a six-storey red sandstone block in the heart of the Merchant City. This former clothing factory, with its exposed stone and brick walls, huge windows, high ceilings and iron stanchions, offered all the essentials for true loft living and the potential to be divided into eighteen shells far bigger – even by Scottish standards – than flats in the same area.

An additional benefit of the site was the adjacent plot, on which MetroLoft is building a modern granite, zinc and galvanized steel extension based on the same principles of height and light, and providing another ten shell apartments.

Spreading the Word   Despite selling units as shells, Andrew realized that it was particularly important to create not just one but two show lofts that – fully fitted out – would demonstrate to an uninitiated Glaswegian audience the fabulous possibilities of loft living. To this end he commissioned two Glasgow architectural practices to design interiors in markedly different styles. Circus and Zoo took a cool, soft, modern approach, with elegant cream and yellow walls, blond, natural materials

and light, spare furniture, while Graven Images went to town with wild colours, quirky fittings and kitsch furniture.

Unashamedly 'in your face', the Graven Images interior in the original Todd building is designed to be memorable. Although one of the smaller spaces, at only 73m² – its modest size relative to the other units – is belied by the grand and opulent treatment that made its unveiling the focus of much press attention. Andrew doubts that the deep purple paint used throughout the interior is a bestseller, but there is no question that, contrasted with a rich mustard colour, the effect is stunning – as Andrew says, 'the combination is difficult to describe, but looks fantastic'.

A similarly theatrical colour scheme had been used by Graven Images in their refurbishment of the nearby Brunswick Hotel, which Andrew saw and loved: 'I wanted them to bring all that richness to this apartment, but at first they resisted, presenting a sample board that was far too cool and restrained. Their taste had shifted a bit since doing the Brunswick. I had to press them into these excesses, but once the apartment began to take shape, I think they were very happy with it.'

The plan (right) reveals how the architects have skewed the division between the living area and bedroom, thus departing from the stolid rectilinearity of the bare shell. The girder shown above that supports the dividing glass 'wall' (see next page) is cleverly designed to look original.

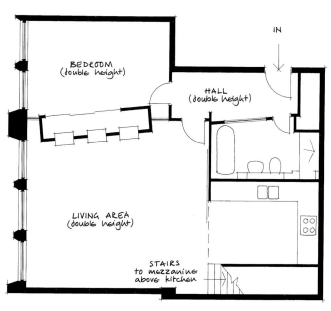

IN

BEDROOM
(double height)

HALL
(double height)

LIVING AREA
(double height)

STAIRS
to mezzanine
above kitchen

Exuberance and Excess   Andrew's own confidence is mirrored in this distinctly tongue in cheek but none the less stylish treatment. With its strong colours, rich textures and witty furniture, the apartment has a kitsch, retro look, but is as inspired by Scottish design – especially the work of Charles Rennie Mackintosh – as by the Pop Art movement and American design of the 1950s.

Visual Witticisms   In the main living area, a space-dividing entertainment 'box' – the most innovative feature of all – is covered in brown wrapping paper, a reference to Mackintosh's use of the same material on the bedroom walls of his Glasgow flat when a student, but also a distinctly post-modern joke about the box being wrapped up, like a gigantic parcel in the middle of the living room. Nor does the fun end there. Centrally positioned, the television niche looks like a fireplace, a visual pun highlighted by the video of a fire that Andrew played throughout the Todd Building launch party.

Neatly parcelling all the electrics into this central entertainment core makes excellent use of the space, avoiding the problem of unsightly wires and the need for ugly cabinets. Throughout the apartment it is this happy combination of lightheartedness and practicality that makes the design so appealing.

The funky brown-paper-wrapped entertainment 'box' (below and right) boldly divides living area from bedroom and provides a wittily post-modern televisual 'hearth'.

Box and Girder   The massive iron girder that runs around the entire living space is both a bold exaggeration of the building's industrial credentials and a structural framework for the internal subdivisions. Supported by – indeed, appearing to hang off – this girder, the 'box' is double-sided, being effectively a divider between the living area and bedroom. Where a wall would chop the space in two, the clear glazed surround of the box makes it possible to see from one room into the other and exposes the entire run of windows, so leaving intact the impressive scale of the original space while retaining the privacy of the bedroom.

The heaviness of the dividing 'box' and the rich, saturated colours of the scheme are offset by light touches, such as the clear glass that flanks the 'box' (left) and the aluminium dining furniture (above).

Fun Furniture   This prominent central feature sets the tone for the correspondingly large and bold furnishings. Luxurious Italian sofas scattered with vibrant cushions face each other over an extraordinary Graven Images-designed footstool-cum-coffee table. Made of an elm log pierced with cavities to hold squash balls, it was originally topped with glass, but when this broke everyone preferred it as the balls were then accessible for *ad hoc* games.

The aluminium café-style dining table and chairs are light and unobtrusive to allow the plane and texture of the oak floor beneath them to be better appreciated. That this flooring extends throughout the whole apartment, uninterrupted by room divisions, again contributes to the feeling of space.

Multi-use space The kitchen area is divided from the main living area by a rolling elm wall (suspended from the girder) so that it can be open to the room or completely sealed off, as desired. A small mezzanine platform above this kitchen offers another flexible solution in this area of the apartment, providing a second sleeping area or study according to the owner's needs.

In many lofts, a mezzanine is a major architectural feature. Here, that role is taken over by the imposing central box, and the mezzanine (above) sits unobtrusively over the kitchen (left), providing a useful sleeping or study area.

The Todd Building brochure observes that these apartments are 'liberated from fixed walls and rigid rooms . . . defined by volume and area, not just by a room count.' And this notion of flexible space – so crucial to the loft aesthetic – is perfectly exemplified by what, if not so deftly handled, could have been a small and uninteresting corner.

A Kitsch Kitchen The creative fusion between Andrew's brief and Graven Images' interpretation is particularly evident in the kitchen itself. Here an eye for the quirky look of the loft led them not to expensive, exclusive suppliers, but to a standard high street store, which happened to have a 'Manhattan' kitchen funkier than anything Andrew or the architects could have hoped for. Even the worktop was a perfect match for the image they were after, having the look of a plastic tray in a 1950s diner. The finished effect is joky and hip, but also very practical and surprisingly expensive-looking, demonstrating that you don't have to spend a fortune to make a loft look good so long as you have imagination and keep an open mind about your sources.

Conspicuous Invention The sumptuous look of this loft stems from the careful choices made in designing it rather than from lashings of cash disbursed. The purpose of a show loft is to demonstrate what can be achieved with a normal budget, and here colour, texture and invention have been cleverly used to replace conspicuous consumption.

The bedroom is a case in point. An ordinary divan bed is dressed with a tasselled bedspread in purple crushed velvet, and a blood red velvet curtain swagged on a scaffolding pole makes a wild and theatrical backdrop for the Graven Images-designed silver-horned Gay Gordon chair. Such seriously over-the-top effects transform what could be an unexceptional room into a boudoir worthy of Cruella de Vil.

Pop Art informs the colours and shapes of this apartment, so an American-style fitted kitchen, with work surfaces resembling plastic diner trays, is entirely in keeping with the architects' desired look.

Opulent textures complement passionate colours in the boudoir-like bedroom, the heavy, swagged velvet curtain making a theatrical statement in what is in fact a modestly sized room. The Graven Images-designed horned chair adds an appropriately surreal touch.

A Revealing Home   In an apartment full of visual statements that make you smile, none is clearer than the glass wall to the bathroom. Only semi-obscure, it shouts – as does the clear glass partition between the living area and the bedroom – that lofts (and this loft in particular) are disinhibiting spaces, encouraging openness, communication and intimacy – not cosy, around-the-fire domesticity, but the sort of closeness that allows you to share everything with someone else.

crystal
palace

**A steel skeleton
with a glass body:
architectural
Utopianism (and
a see-through
bathroom) in
Melbourne,
Australia**

N o art hangs in Bob Nation's Melbourne apartment. The only picture, a photographic seascape, is simply propped up against a wall. Was Bob afraid that artwork would overwhelm the architecture? His response is breathtakingly honest, 'I think it's my own personal arrogance about something made for and by myself, and to hang somebody else's artwork there is inappropriate.' Some might find it inappropriate to live without the soft tones and textures of what might be called 'moderate post-modernism'. But this is Bob's principal home, his private space, and a literal expression of his architectural Utopianism.

Factory Refit   In 1985, with a view to creating an office for Nation Fender Architects, Bob and his wife Tricia, together with the sculptor and jewellery designer Akio and Carlier Makigawa, bought an old furniture factory in the Melbourne suburb of Fitzroy. While Akio and Carlier turned half the space into a studio and apartment, Bob spent five years planning an office with an urban retreat above. Bob remembers, 'It lay in the back of my mind – always something I was going to do – and I carried very abstract ideas of what it could become.'

Bob Nation's belief in the technical versatility of man-made materials has led him to create an open-plan loft (right) where glass and steel predominate. Even the kitchen and shower areas are defined by internal glass ceilings and walls.

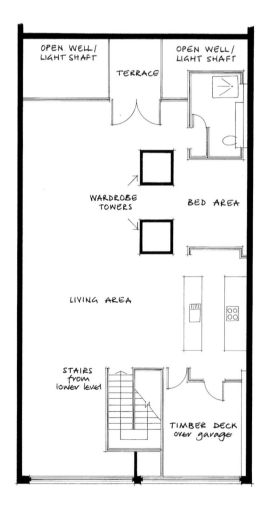

OPEN WELL/
LIGHT SHAFT

OPEN WELL/
LIGHT SHAFT

TERRACE

WARDROBE
TOWERS

BED AREA

LIVING AREA

STAIRS
from
lower level

TIMBER DECK
over garage

Communal or minimal?   Rather than temper the purity of these abstractions, the long gestation period made Bob increasingly determined to realize his architectural dreams. Uncompromised by the pressure of time, he planned a 'major' space, refining – in sketch after sketch – his ideas for a communal area that would be shared with Akio and Carlier. In Highpoint One (see The High Life, pages 30–41) Berthold Lubetkin designed a common lounge and tea room into his apartment block, but since then – even in loft design – shared spaces have largely been avoided. Finally, the pragmatic consideration that the Makigawas would be irritated by Bob's children's music put paid to the idea of a shared space, though the process of considering this idea established the

notion of openness as key to the success of the scheme. As Bob says, 'I have no problem with transparent bathrooms.'

In 1990, when the partners decided to proceed, the pace of the project changed dramatically. Sitting in Bangkok, looking through all the sketches of the previous years ('and deciding it was all kinds of crap', as Bob so pithily remembers), the way forward suddenly became clear: 'There was an obvious answer: structuring the space and making the elements within it as minimal as possible.'

Bob's Glasshouse   Space and light are the main ingredients of most lofts, but here every element of the architecture contributes to their supremacy. Being made exclusively of glass, the walls are effectively windows that block neither the light nor the view. In creating an apartment for himself, Bob felt justified in following his own preference for glass. 'Selfishly, I want to work primarily with glass. I just don't relate to many natural materials.'

Apart from the shape of the space and the pitch of the roof, there is little to suggest that this is a conversion. The oak beams and rugged brickwork that typify London's wharfside lofts are literally and metaphorically thousands of miles from the smooth surfaces and hard

The shining steel and transparent glass structure creates an ever-changing, constantly exciting, visual kaleidoscope of light and texture. Colour and clutter are both banished from this purist palace. The glass of the shower-room walls (above) may be tinted, in a nod towards privacy, but nothing interupts the openness and sense of exposure that characterizes the whole loft.

geometry of Bob's glasshouse home. The approach and the look may be radically different, but there is no doubting Bob Nation's fidelity to an industrial aesthetic, which is intrinsically sympathetic to industrial spaces of all periods.

A Skeleton of Steel Where factory and warehouse builders of the eighteenth and nineteenth centuries used massive wooden beams to support large expanses of floor, Bob uses a contemporary alternative – a steel framework that almost resemble Meccano, on to which the planes of the floors and walls have been attached. Modern as the look may be, the treatment stems from a belief in what is often called 'truth to materials'. Bob observes, 'Steel is more enjoyable when it has a mechanical fix rather than a weld.' And although we may not associate the look with our existing notions of craft, the literal expression of the way the interior has been assembled makes the whole apartment a crafted object – a work of art. As Karl Fender points out, it is a 'piece of art in terms of the craftsmanship that has gone into it'. Bob personally directed the steelworkers so as to ensure that the original design was compromised as little as possible by the building process.

Transparent Living The layout is open and communicative, but zoned to give specific roles to different areas. The bathroom, the only entirely enclosed space, doesn't appear as a small, boxed-off room because its walls – in keeping with the others – are of clear sheets of green-tinted glass. The kitchen is partially enclosed in a steel and glass structure with an open face to the dining area, but again appears entirely open to the main space by virtue of its transparent glass shell. Just as the principal materials

Bob Nation's aesthetic adventure (and his ultimate achievement) is in creating a loft entirely free of domestic norms. Yet all homes need a kitchen and here this is sited within a glazed box that makes it look almost like an art installation.

in the apartment are limited to steel, concrete and glass, so Bob restricted those in the kitchen, using only white or metallic surfaces – most notably stainless steel. Detailing is also kept to a minimum so as to detract as little as possible from the architectonic lines of the white Carrara marble bench top and Gaggenau gas and halogen cooktop.

The principal bedroom has no door but is partially (and practically) screened by two huge flanking wardrobe units that create a grand and elegant portal. One might expect so minimal an environment to look elegant, but that it also looks luxurious comes as a surprise. Here luxury resides not in standard sumptuaries, but in detailing and finish, for example, the custom-designed power points, the subtle changes of flooring (from floorboards to decking) and the occasional use of a particularly distinctive material, such as marble.

Architectural Awards Zinta Jurjans-Heard, the stylist of these photographs, describes the stairs as 'like folded aluminium foil with no visible means of support'. And it is for just such pyrotechnic displays of architectural confidence that the apartment has turned the heads of Australia's architectural fraternity. It has won the Royal Australian Institute of Architects Victorian chapter's Outstanding Architecture Award for residential alterations and additions, the RAIA's National Interior Architecture Award and the Housing Industry Association's Best Residential Alterations, Additions and Renovations Award.

Next Stop: Thailand Bob is rightly proud of his work. In fact, Nation Fender has been appointed the architect of Muang Thong Thani city in Bangkok, a project that, it is envisaged, will eventually house half a million residents. The contrast is striking: a single converted loft space designed to meet Bob Nation's personal needs and tastes to a vast communal housing scheme to suit a population as varied as that of any town. Yet there is a clear connection between the two projects:

the grandeur of their conception. Although no bigger than most lofts (at 340m²), the treatment of this apartment might be described as epic. The clean, post-modern classicism of the structure, the purity of the conception and the sheer confidence of the spatial solutions suggest that this is not just a one-off architectural jewel, but almost a Zen exercise in finding new ways of living. The controlled minimalist aesthetic is infinitely applicable to a larger scheme, and the challenge for Bob Nation now lies in ensuring that half a million people benefit from the lessons learnt in an old factory in the suburbs of Melbourne.

The eye is both baffled and dazzled by the bold yet intricate geometry of a structure (below) in which glass and steel create an Escher-like pattern of level, perspective and plane.

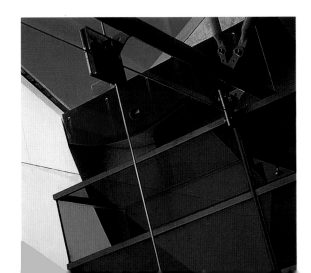

acknowledgements

This book would not have been possible without the kind co-operation of: John Allan, Ou Baholyodhin, Renato Benedetti, Donnathea Bradford, William Broadbent, Gordon Carey, Walter and Mary Adams Chatham, Alison Clark, Elisabetta Cozzi, Freddy Daniels, Julian de Metz, Adalberto del Bo, Tony Goddard, Amit Green, Caroline Haelterman, Harry Handelsman, Rae Hoffenberg, Matthew Jones, Melissa Kojan, Jonathan McDowell, Mac Maclean, Bob Nation, Thierry Oliver, Nik Randall, Barry Sack, Joanna Skoczynska, Nicholas Stuttard, Paul and Su Vaight, Andrew Wadsworth, Erez Yardini.

Thanks are also due to: Zoë Hughes, Caroline Ball, Rosie Anderson and Sarah Bates for their tireless work on the book; and to Dharminder Kang, Claire Nielson, Paul Greenwood, Patricia Owen and Beata Rozekova for their help and encouragement.

Every effort has been made to ensure that the information in this book is correct, and I do hope that no inadvertent errors have crept in.

picture credits

Opening pictures 1, David Churchill, High Drama; 2–3, Richard Glover, Space Invaders; 4–5, Cloud Nine, Curvy Colour.

Introduction 6–7, Gilles de Chabaneix; 8–9, Goddard Manton Architects.

Loft Original 10–17, Scott Frances, Esto Photographics Ltd.

Penthouse Sweet 18–29, Tim Soar (supplied by McDowell & Benedetti).

High Life 30–3, 34–5, 36, 37–41, Thomas Stewart; 34, 36–7, A. C. Cooper (supplied by Avanti Architects).

Curvy Colour 42–3, 45–6, 48, 50–1, Cloud Nine; 47, 49, Brian Harrison; 44, watercolour by John Sibson, computer image by Headingly Estates.

The Top Storey 52–9, Rupert Truman (supplied by Andrew Wadsworth).

Off Beam 60–71, Paul Harmer.

Cool School 72–81, James Macmillan (supplied by Brookes Stacey Randall).

Baroque Bravado 82–91, Tom Lee (supplied by Sapcote Real Lofts).

De Metzanine 92–3, 95, Ed Reeve; 94, 96–101, Chris Tubbs (supplied by De Metz Green Architects).

Milano Magnifico 102–9, Studio Giancarlo Gardin.

Space Invaders 110–13, 114, 114–15, 117–18, 119 (bottom), Tom Craig; 113, 116, 119 (top), Richard Glover (supplied by Circus Architects).

Reservoir Docks 120–9, Paul Harmer (supplied by ECB PR).

Architectural Correctness 130–9, James Macmillan (supplied by Brookes Stacey Randall).

High Drama 140–9, David Churchill.

Crystal Palace 150–7, Earl Carter, Arcaid.

index

Page numbers in *italic* refer to the illustrations